Walking With God

With Toilet Paper
Stuck to my Shoe

A HUMOROUS DEVOTIONAL ABOUT AN
INTIMATE RELATIONSHIP WITH GOD

By
Melissa Jansen

D1158608

TATE PUBLISHING, LLC

Published in the United States of America
by Tate Publishing, LLC
127 East Trade Center Terrace
Mustang, OK 73064
(888) 361–9473

Scripture quotations marked "NLT" are taken from the *Holy Bible, New Living Translation,* copyright © 1996. Used by permission of Tyndale House Publishers, Inc., Wheaton, Illinois 60189. All rights reserved.

The opinions expressed by the author are not necessarily those of Tate Publishing, LLC.

ISBN: 1-9332901-6-1

Dedication

This book is dedicated to my
two beautiful Grandmothers.

Anne M. Mishler
and
A. Anna Folkers

It has always been the highest
kind of compliment to trace
a personal interest, talent,
passion, expression, or feature
back to one of you.
I love you both so much.

Contents

Introduction.. 7

Section One Preview **15**
Barbed-wire Dresses, Stations, and Clean Marsha
Chapter One - Seasons of Life 17
Chapter One Study.. 31
Chapter Two - Identity Crisis............................... 39
Chapter Two Study.. 51
Chapter Three - Eternal Refreshment 57
Chapter Three Study 71

Section Two Preview **79**
Falling in Love, Viagra, and Wal-Mart
Chapter Four - Love Letters.................................. 81
Chapter Four Study... 93
Chapter Five - Vicarious Living 101
Chapter Five Study 115
Chapter Six - Spiritual Senses........................... 123
Chapter Six Study 137

Section Three Preview **145**
Cheeseburgers, Steppingstones, and Tinkle
Chapter Seven - Mixed-Up Thinking 149
Chapter Seven Study... 163
Chapter Eight - Not Enough! 171
Chapter Eight Study.. 183

Chapter Nine - Wisdom Worth Aging For 191
Chapter Nine Study... 201

Section Four Preview **207**
French Fries, Time Outs, and Tight Buns
Chapter Ten - Godly Discipline I.........................211
Chapter Eleven - Godly Discipline II 229
Chapter Twelve - Godly Discipline III 245

Section Five Preview **265**
Boogers, Headless Cockroaches, and a Fried Squirrel
Chapter Thirteen - Surround Yourself................ 269
Chapter Thirteen Study 283
Chapter Fourteen - Get Real 289
Chapter Fourteen Study 305
Chapter Fifteen - Summing It Up 315

Introduction

"**Real** - authentic; genuine. Not pretended; sincere." (Webster's dictionary).

In my relentless pursuit to carry as much guilt as humanly possible, I chose to read a book about motherhood by an author so perfectly clean she must have squeaked as she walked. This woman painted a picture of family life where days were tirelessly filled with games, extra school lessons, Bible memorization, and bedtime stories presented through drama. On top of that, it seemed her lovely lips never parted in a sour word to her husband and, though she didn't say it, I'm convinced that in her entire lifetime she never once had a bad hair day. Reading that book, I remember feeling more and more like a failure with each passing page. *What world does this woman live in?* I wondered as I set fire to the book. *Certainly not mine.*

My husband, Paul, and I took our elementary aged kids to a fast food restaurant for dinner (we're big spenders) recently. Being Friday, Paul was tired after a long week of work. Since I believe Paul should feel revived and uplifted simply by being in my presence, I was feeling irritated with him. On the other extreme, our kids were wound up and unruly for the same reason Paul was tired and listless, it was Friday! And so we set out, for a nice, *relaxing* family night.

Standing in front of the fast food counter, my children laughed out their order as if they were offering a punch line to the hilarious menu. They passed their time by giggling, hitting each other, and spinning circles, until I finally used my most loving voice (HA!) and commanded them to go find a table.

"What do you want honey?" questioned the husband I assumed had made his own bed on the floor by now. "Oh, I'll take a number 3," I said, feeling a headache coming on, " . . . and make it a super size!" This is the equivalent to the alcoholic vice, " . . . and make it a double!"

When the food came I matched each order to its rightful owner and then we said our prayer. Although this prayer was the closest thing to silence I had enjoyed in several hours, I felt it may have been a mistake. Now everyone looking our way would know we belonged to God, thus risking giving God a bad reputation because of the deviant mob we were tonight.

After only one bite from his sandwich and three French fries illegally obtained from his sister, my eight year old son, Ryan, made a brilliant discovery. I found I wasn't much in the mood for brilliant discoveries as I watched Ryan unbutton the top couple buttons of his shirt and lower his straw inside. He put one end of his straw in his mouth and tucked the other into his armpit and proceeded to blow. Oh friends! The loud, juicy sounds that sprang from my son's armpit echoed across the room. Our other two children, Adam and Madison, decided that Ryan might really be on to something, and joined-up with his lively armpit band.

Parents in the booths next to us just smiled. I knew they were inwardly consoling themselves saying, "Well, what do you know, my kids aren't so bad after all." The loud pit-sounds even woke poor departed Paul. So there, in the middle of Arby's, I sat—wondering how my life had fallen to such depths.

Then, unexpectedly, my heavy-eyed Paul perked up as if beckoned by an unearthly calling. He carefully watched the children who were making a mockery of his proud name. Silently, with conviction, he pulled out the straw from his plastic cup and began to play pit-harmony. Ladies, I fell in love again. It turns out my Paulie is quite a gifted armpit-musician!

That Friday night I looked at my family. Each was laughing so hard that occasional things flew aimlessly out their noses, and I thought . . . this is beautiful. Strange—yes, but beautiful. I reflected on the mothering book I had read. The author of that paperback would probably be grabbing for her breather about right now but I guess I'm rather glad I don't live in her world. My world might not be perfect, but it's *real,* and I think I like it. In fact, I know I like it.

God has called me to be "real", just like He's called you to be "real". That doesn't mean we can't dye our hair or get face-lifts; it goes deeper than roots and wrinkles. Being real means *living genuinely.* It means learning and teaching from everyday lessons. It means admitting your struggles and flaws to help someone else glean wisdom from them. It may even mean divulging that certain members of your family occasionally stick straws in their armpits in public.

There's always the temptation of trying to make yourself look good by *pretending* you have it all together. Christians are especially famous for this. Living "real" means you're willing to throw away pretenses and be genuine. It's when we live with this authentic purpose that we are the most effective for Christ.

Some of the antonyms of "real" are words like:

fake, bogus, sham, and phony. Jesus hated that kind of living. To the Pharisees (religious leaders who had themselves perfected counterfeit living), Jesus was seen as some sort of rebel in the way He related to common people on their level instead of using words that made the people feel uneducated and inadequate. Jesus ruffled the Pharisees' robes in the way He so easily connected with, and genuinely cared for, the town riff-raff. He blew away all their illusions of what the Messiah would be like by being . . . well, by being real.

Yes, Jesus was perfect. Yes, Jesus was God; however, "He did not consider equality with God something to be grasped, but made himself nothing, taking the very nature of a servant, being made in human likeness. And being found in appearance as a man he humbled himself and became obedient to death - even death on a cross!" Philippians 2:6–8

Our Jesus was real. He was genuine. Not pretended; sincere. And just as He *is,* so is His relationship intended to be with each of us. He knows all about our past, our insecurities, our struggles - even our morning breath - and yet, He holds out His hand to us like a beaming bridegroom. *I'm grabbing it girls!* ***I'm taking the hand of God and walking with Him wherever He leads me, dragging my imperfections***

like toilet paper stuck to my shoe behind me. He wants the real me.

In this study we'll travel through many diverse topics together but they'll all relate back to this real relationship between Jesus and us. It's my prayer that you'll laugh, think, change, and mature as we trudge our way through.

The chapters are set up just for you in an individual study, or you can grab a girlfriend or two (or three or four) and use it as a group study. At the end of each chapter you'll find clusters of questions. The first set is called; "Getting to know you . . ." These will be useful in a group setting to help the ladies get better acquainted. In a personal setting they'll be fun in the way they rekindle some old memories and new thoughts. These questions will lead you into the next set entitled, "It's time to apply!"

"It's time to apply!" are questions that will help you think deeper about how the subject-at-hand applies to your life. These will naturally prepare you for the last section which will be "Journaling." Here you'll answer questions that are a little more personal and are meant to prepare you for prayer. A simple praise-prayer is written to start off your time of prayer, then followed by plenty of journaling space.

The last activity in the journaling section is something I'm both excited and nervous about. The apostle Paul writes in 2 Corinthians 13:13, "May the *grace* of our lord **Jesus Christ**, the *love* of **God,** and the *fellowship* of the **Holy Spirit** be with you all." This verse describes the distinct characteristics of the Trinity; God the Father, the Holy Spirit, and Jesus Christ the Son. I'm excited to set aside a journaling space aimed at distinguishing the intimate, daily involvement of the Trinity in our lives. This is also where my nervousness sprouts. I'm nervous that the whole "Trinity-thing" will seem too daunting and some may choose to skip over it. Don't skip it! When you get to this section, ***instead of focusing on what you don't understand,*** simply close your eyes and look at what God is doing within you—and admire Him. Grab hold of any truth you've gleaned from the lesson and ask God to show you, remind you, and refine you.

"Trust in the Lord with all your heart;
do not depend on your own understanding.
In all your ways acknowledge him, and
he will make your paths straight."
Proverbs 3:5

Reading through these chapters, I'm sure you'll find them to be rather simple and often quirky, but I hope you'll always find them real. After all, that's the world Jesus lived in. That's the world I live in. Don't you?

So, if you like, turn the page and get started. For added pleasure, grab a straw and play a few songs while you read. It's actually kind of relaxing. Go ahead, hit it maestro!

~ Melissa Jansen

Section One

Barbed-wire dresses, Stations, and "Clean Marsha"

As I have already stated, I live in a house with other people. The people include my husband, Paul; my sons, Adam and Ryan; and my daughter, Madison.

Growing up, I'd hoped to live in a house with a family like this one but I somehow forgot to imagine the countless toys on the floor, the unflushed toilets, or the landmass of laundry. No, those little perks are the unexpected blessings called "real life". You think life is going to pan out picture-perfect and then . . . Splat! Reality. Like bird poop on the windshield, it kind of spoils the view.

In this first section we'll explore how our attitude toward the reality on our windshield affects our relationship with Jesus Christ. Throughout the seasons of this life we'll find God stationing us in areas that can either add character and wisdom, or bitterness and self pity, to our moral fiber. Some days the jury is still out on which ones I personally am adding.

So, whether you're finding yourself today with a stubborn heart (Chapter One), an identity crisis (Chapter Two), or a dehydrated spirit (Chapter Three), I'm sure you'll see you're not alone as you pass through these pages. Oh, I'm so excited to get started . . . pardon me for just a second though, I need to go wipe off my windshield.

Chapter One

SEASONS OF LIFE

*"There is a time for everything,
a season for every activity under heaven."*

Ecclesiastes 3:1

While growing up in Decatur, Indiana, I watched a group of men perform a drama about the seasons of life—in the form of a wonderful, tear-jerking song. I'll never forget it.

First, a small boy walked out on a dark stage

and stood in the single spotlight. He sang about the springtime of life: catching frogs and other carefree, whimsical moments from childhood. I was only twelve but I remember sitting there sighing, "Hummm . . . where has my Springtime gone?"

Next, came out a boy in his early teens. This was Summer. I smiled each time his solo was punctuated by occasional pubescent squeaks. It had to be hard to find a young man secure enough to stand in front of his peers and sing, "I am the summer days," while his own voice wrestled with the decision of being a man or a child. His verse touched on the mystery of girls and other tantalizing, tortured moments of adolescence. The entire audience was captivated.

Then, out came Autumn. He was man in his forties who sang with experience and grace. Autumn's words told about his role in the family and the changes he felt in his aging body. As I sat there mesmerized, I could hear sniffling noses throughout the congregation.

I realize that to fully appreciate some moments you just have to be there. Maybe this moment was one of those. It's hard to convey the emotions that swept across the crowd that night. Even though the music was swelling, it felt strangely quiet as Winter slowly crossed the stage.

Tears dropped into my lap while I watched the

elderly gentleman make his way through the darkness to the small circle of light that had already embraced the previous seasons of life. When he finally reached the microphone he had to lean against his cane to catch his breath. A faint smile spread across his mouth while the spotlight illuminated the years on his face. At just the right moment Winter wet his lips and began to sing in a worn, wise voice about aging. His lyrics were simple yet powerful. Earlier I chuckled as summer's voice cracked with the beginnings of manhood. Now I cried listening to winter's voice crack with the effects of drawing near the end.

This simple song was such a moving experience because it presented the ecstasy, agony, and irony of aging. The audience certainly saw the inevitable decline of the body, yet we also felt the invisible strengthening of the soul. It wasn't as depressing as it might sound. It was more like watching a travelogue featuring a trip everyone knew they were destined to take but not sure how to feel about it . . . or what to pack.

Looking back on that day, it's sobering to find myself now in a completely different season. I have such a love/hate relationship with time. I love the new experiences that time brings; yet, I hate how quickly time goes by. Just as I get settled into one season, I find myself entering the next one. Time is the ultimate thief because it steals away our days, carelessly leaving incriminating evidence behind (like crows feet, gray hair and sagging skin), and yet we just can't seem to catch it!

Compartmentalizing our lives into four convenient sections, as with the "seasons of life" terminology, isn't realistic for most people. You might be a forty-year-old Spring or even a twenty-year-old Autumn. No matter what season you find yourself experiencing, God has a plan for you. He has intentionally delivered you to this day according to His purposes. You are never too young or too old to be used.

Just as our temporary bodies change with the passing of time, so do the areas God places us for His work. I'll be referring to these areas as "stations." For instance, my dad was *stationed* in Korea for part of his military career (and he has the slides to prove it, should you ever be interested.). He was sent to a specific spot to fulfill the commitment he made to his country. The army would not have sent a child there, nor an eighty-year-old man. My dad's age, circumstances, and training were considered and aligned with this assignment.

God has assigned you today to a station. The season of life you're in, your circumstances, and your training may play a part in this assignment. If you're a Mother, that's a station. If you're a wife, that's a station. Teacher? Nurse? Student? These are all stations that God wants to use you in for His glory.

Some stations are not so pleasant. You may be facing an assignment that you don't feel equipped to face. Maybe you've just found out you have cancer or that your teenaged daughter is pregnant. These are difficult situations, and my heart breaks for you if this is your case, but I do know that God can use you there. I don't write that to be cute and upbeat, I write it because Scripture give us scores of examples of God's people in horrendous situations being used in exquisite ways. If however, and I must say this, you find yourself in an unsafe situation, such as abuse, I don't believe God has called you to stay and endure it. Leave, get help and ask for guidance.

Season - Commonly refers to age. You are considered in the Spring, Summer, Autumn, or Winter season of your life. Seasons are constantly changing.

Station - The roles we fill because of the people and things we find ourselves surrounded by. Stations often change with the changing of our seasons.

We'll be hashing and rehashing the "season"

and "station" subjects in these first three chapters because I believe they are at the core of how a woman sees herself. In my years of working with women, I'm amazed at how a station or season of life often serves as an excuse for not entering new opportunities for the Lord. There have been many times I've had older women opt not to share in a group setting because she's convinced no one would be interested in what someone her age would have to say. Isn't that sad? A wealth of wisdom hidden under a rock. I've also seen young mothers blush while trying to explain how someday, when their kids are older, they'll be able to get involved in a ministry of some kind. Sweet Mommy, what could possibly be a more vital ministry than pouring your life into the children God has entrusted to you? Yes, *someday* you may be able to add additional ministry opportunities, but *today* you are being marvelously used.

Don't use your station, or season, as an excuse.

Embrace it with a passionate focus.

The devil loves to rob us of purpose and make us feel powerless. Take a minute right now and ask God to show you the place(s) He has stationed you and commit to glorify Him through it in a fresh new way.

Read God's bold words through Paul in Colossians 3:23–24 telling us how we are to work effectively in the places He has stationed us.

> *"Whatever you do, work at it with all your heart, as working for the Lord, not for men, since you know that you will receive an inheritance from the Lord as a reward."*

You might as well know something about me right now in Chapter One. Nothing biblical comes easy to me. For instance, I exhibit a real talent for judging people, and yet, God tells me I'm not supposed to judge. I was born a gifted smart-aleck, and yet, God tells me to hold my tongue. So, it only makes sense that this verse goes against my nature as well.

At first glance we may interpret this Colossians verse as a call to successfully work with our hands wherever God has stationed us. I can do that. Ahhh, but what this verse *actually* asks of us is to work successfully with our hearts, and that's a whole new nature! God sees past our outer offerings and peeps right into the attitude of our heart. No fair.

I once worked for a man I had little respect for. He wasn't vulgar, grossly immoral, or a law-breaker. This man just seemed to have a knack for being annoying. I wasn't the only employee who felt irritated—we all did. He was an "equal opportunity annoyer".

The easiest way for me to make it through the day was to commit to avoid eye contact and conversation with my boss as much as possible. Now, in some situations this may have been the best answer for the problem but in my situation it only made it worse. My attitude was ugly and, to be really honest, somewhere inside of me I started to view myself as superior to him. Not superior as in "higher-ranking" at the office, I felt "higher-ranking" as a person! The regaling of unflattering boss-stories with co-workers only worsened this attitude and an eerie appetite grew within me for more and more to complain about. It was like growing fat on mud. My belly felt full and satisfied by injesting rot.

Colossians 3:23–24 was brought to my attention by my husband. He's a brave man, that Paul. My work-attitude (which had started to spread into other areas of my life) made me feel sick when I saw how far I was from the Truth and I committed myself to change -and change I did!

My disposition at work immediately improved and my boss found me a more polite person to work with. I smiled daily and even managed to make sounds resembling laughter at his attempts at humor. Believe it or not, I even purged the habit of sharing unflattering boss-stories with my co-workers, even when I was given fresh, quality material to share. My outer offerings were steadily becoming strong and healthy! My inner offerings, however, were comatose and on life-support. You see, my real problem wasn't the *working of my hands;* it was the *working of my heart.* Inside, I was the same groveling mud-eater; I had just learned to feast alone.

Colossians 3:23–24 tells us to be willing to work for, or serve, undeserving people the same way we would work for, or serve, our always deserving God—wherever He has stationed us. Outward attempts at appearing servant-hearted never fool our Lord and only hinder His transforming work within us. A powerful witness in our station(s) starts with a humble heart that's willing to serve people whether they're considered rich, poor, least, greatest, charming, or annoying.

Speaking of committing to those who may not deserve to be served, let's look at the station of being a wife and mother. My friend Shelly shared a story with me over a piece of hot fudge cake that illustrates this point perfectly.

It seems that Shelly and her husband, Rob, had promised to rearrange their two daughters' bedroom. On a slow Saturday afternoon, while the girls were off playing, Shelly decided it was the perfect time for cleaning and room rearranging. Rob had other ideas. He decided it was the perfect time to curl up on the couch for a nap . . . leaving Shelly alone with her ambition.

Being the kind, generous woman that she is, Shelly decided to get started on the cleaning while her beloved enjoyed a little siesta. She washed dishes, swept the floor, and did a general tidying up until she figured Rob would surely be awake. Instead, as she slaved, Rob continued to selfishly slumber. Shelly was left to do what all good wives do when they want to awaken their husband "unintentionally"—she revved up the vacuum cleaner! It was the perfect answer for her dilemma. She could wake-up Rob and still come off as the busy, doting housewife. However, the vacuum was no match for Rob. He was a champion napper.

My normally gentle friend was getting plenty ticked off. Afterall, Rob knew her plans to get this work done and he knew she needed his help! Passing the couch on her way to the girls' bedroom, Shelly poured a cold cup on sarcasm on his head saying, "Hey, Rob, don't worry, I'll do this myself. Please, just stay on the couch; I wouldn't want to trouble you."

In the bedroom, Shelly bent down to look under the beds and realized why Betsy and Erin had been able to "clean" their rooms so quickly lately.

Toys and clothes filled the bed's underbelly like cream in a Twinkie. *Ungrateful kids!* thought Shelly while getting on all fours to scrape out the rubble. With half her body ingested by the steel jaws of the bed frame she yelled out, "Please, Rob, get your rest! No, I'm sure I won't hurt my back if I move the beds by myself! As long as you're happy . . . that's all I care about!"

Shelly and I snickered into our hot fudge cake about her all-too-familiar story. At my house, there are times when Paul marinates himself in the couch cushions while I work on everything from dinner to world peace. I get steamed up because he doesn't think to come help me but there's NO way I'm going to ask him for help. He should just know I need it! By the time dinner is served I've decided to never let him touch me again. I've become a self-proclaimed martyr, working with my hands while my heart whines and complains.

My pal Shelly said it best while concluding her story that night. "You know, at the time I really felt I was doing the right thing. I was working. I was serving my family. The whole time though, I was feeling more and more angry about how none of them deserve all the work I do. My attitude was anything but servant like."

The truth is, whether it's your husband, children,

boss, or friend, it's hard to work for people who don't deserve our efforts. God isn't bent on pummeling His children down to a doormat status; He just wants us to learn to serve without any strings attached. He wants us to be so committed to the stations He's given us that we're willing to discipline ourselves to work as though we're working for God.

Serving unselfishly changes lives. Jesus called it "dying to self"—inviting Christ to become more and more, while making ourselves less and less. It's a paradox, but we will truly experience greater fulfillment by yielding our will, than we ever could by demanding our own way.

Sophia Loren once said that a woman's dress should be like a barbed-wire fence; it should serve its purpose without obstructing the view. Isn't that wonderful? What an excellent illustration of how we are called to serve our Lord in the stations He places us while passing through the seasons of this life. **With style and grace we are to serve without obstructing other's view of God.** Our purpose should be to work to our fullest potential, with our hands and our hearts, for His glory, not our own.

Paul wrote this to the church in Thessalonica, and all believers everywhere:

> *"And so we keep on praying for you, that our God will make you worthy of the life*

*to which he called you. And we pray that
God, by his power, will fulfill all your
good intentions and faithful deeds. Then
everyone will give honor to the name of
our Lord Jesus because of you, and you
will be honored along with him. This is all
made possible because of the undeserved
favor of our God and Lord, Jesus Christ."*

God has given you a station in life; strive to glorify Him through it.

It isn't too early or too late to live a life of purpose
and fulfillment. You don't have to wait until you can
go somewhere special or spare a certain amount of
time. Start today, wherever you are stationed, in
whatever season. Be willing to serve those who don't
deserve it (that's everybody, by the way). Invite God
to become more while you become less—and, above
all, go out and buy a barbed-wire dress.

Seasons of Life

Chapter One Questions

Getting to know you, getting to know all about you . . .

1. What song makes you feel reminiscent?

2. What season (Spring, Summer, Fall, Winter) of life *are* you in? What season do you *feel* like you're in?

3. Of the seasons you've passed through, do you have a favorite? Which one?

It's time to apply!
God has given you a station right now.
Strive to glorify Him through it.

Look up these verses and write the main thought in the space provided. Note what they say about serving others.

Galatians 5:13 -

Ephesians 2:10 -

4. Where are you stationed right now? Do you feel equipped?

5. How are you allowing God to change the world around you through your station?

6. In your station(s), are you a servant with your hands? With your heart?

> The ultimate ambition is to embrace
> *who* and *where* we are *today*
> with a passionate focus,
> ready to ***serve without reserve***
> for the glory of our Lord.

7. Do you have a reservation, Mam? Not for dinner, for service. It could be your age, education, knowledge of the Bible, weight, time limits, marital status, ability to have children, etc. What holds you back from saying,

"Yes!" to a new opportunity or "Yes!" to giving yourself completely to your station right now?

8. Has anyone ever served you with no reserve? Who? What stands out about that experience?

Journaling Time

Look up these verses and write the main thought in the space provided:

Colossians 3:23–24 -

Philippians 2:14 -

Ephesians 4:2 -

Ephesians 4:31 -

Who is the hardest person for you to work for with all your heart, as if you are working for God - for His glory alone? Why?

What will you do today to change the attitude of your heart to that of a servant?

Are you willing to make that change(s) if ***everything else stays the same around you?***

"Your attitude should be the same as Christ Jesus had. Though he was God, he did not demand and cling to his rights as God. He made himself nothing; he took the humble position of a slave and appeared in human form. And in human form he obediently

humbled himself even further by dying a criminal's death on a cross." Philippians 2:5–8L

Let's Pray . . .

How can I ever thank You for the way You came to this earth, being the omnipotent God, and yet taking the very station of a common man. *You served the people around You with Your hands and the people were amazed. You served the people around You with Your heart and the people were changed.*

Thank You Lord, for being so humble, so loving.

Father, today I learned this:

Holy Spirit, remind me this week of these things:

Jesus, our relationship will benefit from these changes because:

Chapter Two

IDENTITY CRISIS

*"Jesus Christ is the same yesterday
and today and forever."*

Hebrews 13:8

In the previous chapter we talked about seasons and stations and how essential it is to place our primary focus on the working of our heart rather than the working of our hands. We're called to work for seemingly undeserving people as if we were working for God. What a challenge!

In this chapter, we're continuing to look at these stations and how they often change or redefine with age. Old responsibilities may be replaced with new ones as our spring, summer, autumn, and winter days blow in and blow out.

For mothers, some of the hardest changes can be connected with our children. I remember the day I sent off my youngest child, Madison, for her first day of kindergarten. The big, yellow bus opened its doors and swallowed up my kids one at a time, leaving me alone with a heart full of gravel and a deep, thirsty feeling inside. I was like a ship that had been christened, proclaimed ready to sail, without any destination in mind.

I'm not going to lie to you; I was excited about being a free woman for a few hours. I had been fantasizing for years about having coffee with my friends at quaint little places full of breakables. Even the thought of a nice, hot bath without any interruptions sounded like bliss. Shopping without potty breaks every ten minutes, going through a check-out line without buying blue-slime candy, not searching for children hiding inside the clothes racks—**all** these things sounded fabulous to me. Yet, as only a mother can understand, I felt a longing to get someone a drink or tie some shoes. But the six little feet I love the most just rode off, in the belly of a bus, without me.

During my first officially free morning, I walked into my quiet bedroom and pulled out a drawer of my desk. In a stack of wrinkled papers, I found something I had written years before. I hardly remembered writing it and wasn't impressed by its quality, but the theme certainly fit my mood at that particular moment. It's simply called "Shoes."

* * * * *

As I walk through the clutter in my house, I'm amazed at how quickly my three small children and I can mess things up! My younger two are quietly tucked away for a much treasured nap while I gather, throw away, and straighten up the items littering my floors and counter tops.

I see one of my daughter's tiny sandals and, without much thought, pick it up and search for the mate. Another of her shoes lies cockeyed in the corner but it doesn't belong to the first. After a brief search, I find the mates to both shoes and carry them to the stairs. Just as I am about to lay them down, those four little shoes catch my eye—and my heart. They're so tiny that I have all four of them in one hand! I can almost hear the precious sound of her little one-year-old feet pitter-patting across the floor.

Seasoned mothers have reminded me how quickly time goes by. I know that in no time at all, my daughter and her shoes will do a great deal of changing. She'll go from little white sandals that show off her tiny, stubby toes to sleek, white high heels that carry her down the aisle on her daddy's arm. The only thing sure to stay the same, at least for several more years, is finding all those shoes lying around the house!

I'm convinced that our precious Lord gives us things such as stray shoes as sweet little reminders of where he has "stationed" us right now. Whose shoes are you tripping over in this portion of your life? Maybe you're stumbling over those great, big basketball shoes that you had to mortgage the house to buy for your teenage son. As you're falling to the floor, ask yourself if you've told him lately how much you appreciate him.

Maybe you're finding your daughter's ballet slippers stuffed behind the pillows of the couch. They're pink, which means they match the newest color of her hair. You know, she loves it when you sit down and really listen to her.

Maybe you find your husband's huge work boots at the end of a muddy trail. Remind yourself how blessed you are to have a partner who faithfully goes to work each day and comes home to his family each night.

Or perhaps you're at the stage of life where you're only bending down to pick up your own shoes. At times, maybe you actually long to find someone else's slippers, boots, sandals, or muddy tennies parked under your coffee table. Your mind reviews memories when the house was filled with the sound of busy feet. Now, it's quiet. Friend, be delighted that God has not forgotten you; He hasn't run out of uses for you. He still has dreams for you and can't wait to see you get out of bed and put on those wonderful slippers of yours. No matter what station you're in - no matter what shoes you find or hope to find - remember that you are a treasure when your feet (and heart) belong to God.

Romans 10:15 says, "How beautiful are the feet of those who bring good news!"

I believe that the Lord loves to see the shoes of His children scattered here and there after they've been walking around sharing and living His love with all those around them.

Oh these little, precious shoes. I think I'll just hold them for a while! It's amazing that there are days with my children that seem so very long, but the years pass by all too quickly.

* * * * *

Of all mornings to find that paper! I thought I was going to have to skip coffee and just head to the stress center when I realized I had written that over four years ago. Where had the time gone? When did Madison grow so big? How long had it been since I'd cleaned out my drawers?

I plopped down on my bed and wondered what I'd be doing when I blink again and send my kids off to junior high, high school, and college. Even more important, "*Who* would I be?" I felt strangely like I had found a new me and lost the old me all on the same morning. I kept checking my shirt for a nametag—*Who am I*? *After years of defining myself as a stay-at-home mommy, I'd watched my kids ride away that morning with a big piece of my identity.* **Who am I?**

Do not define yourself by what station or season you are in.

There are countless ladies checking their shirts for name tags every day. They've lost their job, their husband (to death or divorce), or their youthful beauty, and they don't have a clue who they are anymore. In times like these it's normal to feel suddenly confused or lost, but hopefully these will bring us to a point of reassessment with God. **Passing stations and seasons**

**serve as excellent reminders to check where our
identity is invested.**

Again, we are called to glorify God wherever
He has placed us. However, and this is where it gets
tricky, we must be careful not to draw our identity or
self-worth from our station. There is a thin, dangerous
line between *nurturing* a role or job and *becoming*
that role or job. Doing your best is godly, but to lose
yourself (which is worship) in a station is sin. It's
idolatry.

In Luke 9:25 Jesus asks, "What good is it for
a man to gain the whole world and yet forfeit his (or
her) very self?"

The problem with allowing our identity to rest
in a station or season of life, no matter how wonderful
it is, is that nothing this world has to offer is eternal
outside of relationships with and through Jesus Christ.
**We were created in the image of an eternal God
with eternal purposes for us. We were not created
to define ourselves through temporary sources.**

Earthly stations and seasons
are temporary. Invest eternally.

As a kid, my parents warned me about the
devil's underhanded game of using good, unexpected
things in our lives as an attention sponge to soak all

our focus up and leave little-to-nothing for God. These days my attention is spread thinly in every direction, like a little jelly on a big piece of toast, I certainly see this as truth. I spend my day focusing on all the temporary work around me, even though it's good to take care of my stations, and neglect to focus on my eternal God and what He's doing around me.

2nd Corinthians 4:18, "So we fix our eyes not on what is seen, but on what is unseen. For what is seen is temporary, but what is unseen is eternal."

The devil wants to break, divide, and destroy our personal relationship with God in any way we allow him. (1 Peter 5:8) While we may guard our heart against pride, lust and other obvious threats, we are often oblivious to more subtle dangers. Allowing our days to fill up with temporary stuff to the point that we don't have the time or energy to invest in the eternal is one way we can fall into the devil's devious grip. Satan doesn't care if he defeats us through a drug addiction or a busy-lifestyle addiction . . . as long as he defeats us. When our exhausting routine is allowed to alienate us from God, the devil can slide in other temptations that we are too weak to fight.

Many nights, as I slip my tired toes down deep into my cozy bed sheets, I can't shake a feeling that I've forgotten to do something. My mind reviews my hectic day and I remember not *what* I forgot, but **whom** I forgot—God. I failed to spend any time with my Lord! I pray and try to make excuses: Lord, it's just been such a busy day. I haven't had a spare moment. Then the Holy Spirit gently reminds me that I had enough time to fit in my shower and make-up; my errands and friends. I somehow had the time to run the kids around, care for the house, fix dinner, and watch television. I fit in all this and more, yet mysteriously, I couldn't spare any precious moments for my Heavenly Father. I managed to juggle all sorts of temporary things while I clumsily dropped the eternal.

So what's the answer? Should we stop driving the kids around? Is spending time with our friends too frivolous? Is God wanting us to stop bathing? No! The answer is found in Matthew 6:33 as it reminds us to "Seek first His (God's) kingdom and His (God's) righteousness, and all these things (our daily needs) will be given to us as well." When our priority is God and what He has for us today, all the temporary stuff will fall into place.

Speaking of mixed-up priorities, do you remember the story of that biblical domestic duo, Mary and Martha? If not, turn to Luke 10:38–42 and you will peek into Martha's (they don't tell her last name but her attitude suggests it might be Stewart) kitchen. In the passage, Martha is rushing around the kitchen as she checks on the roast, salts the mashed potatoes, and folds the napkins in the shape of little fishies. It's a big day; she's invited Jesus and the boys over for dinner and everything needed to be just right! Can you blame her?

This story might not have found its way into scripture if not for a little something else Martha was cooking up in her kitchen that day - a great big pot of hostility. You see, while Martha was running around on her aching feet, her sister Mary was plopped down on a rug, listening to Jesus and laughing with the boys. Can't you just see Martha peeking around the kitchen corner trying to get Mary's attention with those flesh-burning glares only sisters can give? Mary looked at her and motioned, "Just a minute, I'm coming . . . Hey, Jesus, tell me what it means to be re-born."

Well, Martha finally has had all she can stand! Running out to the center of her reclining guests, she looks at Jesus with wet-stress in her eyes and dramatically demands, "Lord, don't you care that my sister has left me to do the work by myself? Tell her to help me!"

The disciples' mouths dropped open at the sudden theatrical display and everyone looked at Jesus . . . including Mary, who was feeling *very* embarrassed. "Martha, Martha," the Lord calmly answered, "you are worried and upset about many things, but only one thing is needed. Mary has chosen what is better, and it will not be taken away from her."

The Bible doesn't record what happened next, but I have enough sibling experience to know that Mary stuck her tongue out at Martha. Not long enough for Jesus to see . . . just a quick, "So there!" for Martha to treasure.

Poor Martha gets such a bad reputation for something we're all guilty of. Who hasn't chosen to get tangled up in the temporary while neglecting the eternal? Martha was so blinded by her temporary station that she failed to see an eternal opportunity.

Although we're called to work in our assigned areas selflessly for eternal purposes, we're not called to lose our identity in the process. **It's imperative to our continued growth as women-claimed-eternal, to invest in our God Who knows *who we were, who we are, and who we will be.*** Time spent centered in Him, renews us, refreshes us (our next chapter!), and gives us purpose.

I love the season and stations I'm in right now. I love the ages of my children. I love having Paul as my husband. I'm committed to being the most effective mommy and wife I can be. I'm mindful, however, that these stations are not permanent. If these temporary roles which are so precious to me are ever taken away, I know I will still be a woman of value because *my identity is in Jesus Christ and not in my temporary stations of life.*

If you are a Christian woman, your identity is not in this temporary life—it is in the eternal Life-giver. Our relationship with God through Jesus Christ is the most powerful, fruitful and exciting adventure we could ever experience. It's out of this relationship that our stations are blessed eternally and it's this relationship that requires our first priority. We need to invest ourselves eternally.

So woman, live ABUNDANTLY today remembering that the Lord is a God of purpose. He loves you with purpose and He leads you with purpose. As you meet with Him daily you will find that you are much more than your station and season.

Perhaps God leads us through things that are constantly changing *to remind us that He never will!*

Identity Crisis

Chapter Two Questions

Getting to know you, getting to know all about you . . .

1. Who is the messiest person in your home? Why do you give them that title?

      1a. If you live alone, are you a messy person or a neat freak?

2. Do you like to shoe shop? What's your favorite shoe store?

3. Who was your kindergarten teacher? Did you like him or her?

It's time to apply!

Do not define yourself by what station or season you are in.

Season - Commonly refers to age. You are considered in the Spring, Summer, Autumn, or Winter season of your life. Seasons are constantly changing.

Station - The roles we fill because of the people and things we find ourselves surrounded by. Stations often change with the changing of our seasons.

Tell what station or season these men and women identified with and how it made them feel toward the plans God had for them. You may need to read a few verses before and after these listed scriptures if you are not familiar with the story.

Luke 1:34 -

Genesis 18:11–12 -

4. Have you ever defined yourself by a season or station? What was it?

5. What's the harm of defining ourselves with temporary things?

6. What can you do to make sure that a station or season in your life doesn't consume you? What boundaries might you need to make?

Sometimes other people will define you by your season or station. Read these scripture verses and record how this happened to some of our favorite biblical characters as well.

1 Samuel 17:32–33 -

Luke 5:27–29 -

Matthew 13:53–57

7. Have other people defined you by your station or season? How?

Journaling Time

Keeping in mind that God loves you tremendously, how do you think He would define you?

Is your relationship with the Lord powerful, fruitful, and exciting? Give a specific example of how you have experienced each of these characteristics.

Powerful:

Fruitful:

Exciting:

If you are having trouble with that, what might you

need to change or invest to experience God Powerfully, Fruitfully, and with great Excitement!?

Let's Pray . . .

Lord, I'm not sure if I got your nose, eye shape, or dimples when you created me in Your magnificent image, but I do know You've made me a reflection of Your eternal self. I wasn't made for temporary purposes! I was made to bring You praise for an eternity. Give me wisdom and strength to do that today - wherever You have called me. I love You.

Father, today I learned this:

Holy Spirit, remind me this week of these things:

Jesus, our relationship will benefit from these changes because:

Chapter Three

ETERNAL REFRESHMENT

"The Lord will guide you always; He will satisfy your needs in a sun-scorched land and will strengthen your frame. You will be like a well-watered garden, like a spring whose waters never fail."
Isaiah 58:11

Across the street from my house are two homes filled up with two different families. To protect the innocent, I'll call them the Smiths and the Joneses. The ladies I will describe to you are wonderful gals and I truly love them. This story simply pokes fun at the areas in which they excel and I neglect. Let's start with Marsha Smith.

Marsha Smith is wonderful. She and her husband have no children and their house looks it; everything is always in place. For instance, one time I went over to borrow some vanilla from Marsha and as Marsha opened her pantry door it was as if a bright heavenly light shone out upon me and the angels of heaven began to sing.

"It's . . . it's beautiful," was all I could get to come out of my throat.

Marsha smiled knowingly and said, "Thanks, it's alphabetized."

As Marsha went to the "V" section and handed me the vanilla, I felt embarrassed about my pantry at home. I couldn't possibly alphabetize my spices because all their labels have fallen off. Besides, they're all cemented to the shelves with the Karo Syrup I spilled about two years ago.

I thanked "Clean Marsha." As I crossed the street, I apologized to the vanilla for what it was about to see. The poor spice was used to tidiness and order - but now - for the first time, it was headed for the other side of the road. The side where naked dishes lay dirty and used in the sink for days and where silverware is found abandoned and left for dead in the cracks of the couch. When I carried the pampered vanilla into my kitchen I could almost hear its little flavorful voice saying, "Oh . . . my . . . goodness!—Please, don't hurt me."

Next door to Marsha lives Laura Jones. Although she has three children, Laura works outside the home. It seems that anytime I see her she is dressed in head-to-toe fashion. "Lovely Laura" is beautiful, with her rich dark skin and shiny, black hair. To complete the picture, the aroma of her incredible cooking spills out her kitchen window and leaves every tongue in our neighborhood wagging.

Then there's me. As I've said, my house doesn't compare to "Clean Marsha's." And, I must now confess, my wardrobe doesn't stand a chance against "Lovely Laura's." Because I work at home, I've gotten in the habit of throwing on something comfortable for the day. In fact, sometimes I'll wear what was comfortable the day before. I roll out of bed, look at what is lying on the floor beside me and I say, "Congratulations dirty shirt and ripped shorts! It's your lucky day - maybe even your lucky week!"

I guess I had sort of fallen into what might be described as a rut in my wardrobe when I fell in love with a cut-off pair of overalls. Day after day, I picked them off my floor and buckled their faithful arms over my shoulders. Those overalls became like family to me. I even made wallet-sized pictures of them to pass out at Christmas. They traveled through nearly every day with me without complaining or demanding. What dedication.

One day, while wearing my bibs, I saw "Clean Marsha" by my mailbox. Being the friendly girl I am, I went out to say, "hi." As we were talking, over came "Lovely Laura" wearing—were my eyes deceiving me?—sweatpants! I had never seen Laura wear anything as casual as sweats and I couldn't help but remark, "Laura, you're wearing sweat pants!"

The statement brought a blank look to "Lovely Laura's" face.

"I mean," I continued, "you're always dressed up. Now you look casual—like me. I always wear these," I said, pointing awkwardly at my beloved overalls.

"Clean Marsha" cut in, "You know, you *do* always wear those."

Instantly, as I watched Marsha's lips moving and her nose scrunching up as she talked, I felt a thick blanket of insecurity and embarrassment cover me. Sure, *I* was already aware that I wore these bibs a lot but I didn't realize *the neighbors* were on to me!

Without bothering to stop and breathe, Marsha plunged on, "But I was thinking about it the other day (Great! She THINKS about my overalls in her spare time!), and I figure with all your kids you must have so much laundry that you don't have time to do your own!"

At this point, if I had been a turtle, my head would have been firmly tucked into my shell. In fact, I tried to stick my head down into my bibs but a rat in my hair was stuck on the buckle. I was feeling very inadequate to be in the presence of "Clean Marsha."

Sensing the awkwardness, I believe, "Lovely Laura" tried to change the subject by saying, "Hey Marsha, I'm thinking of going back to college for another degree."

Marsha turned her scrunched-up nose away from me and said to Laura, "Oh, not me, I'm already **way** over qualified for my job."

As they continued their conversation, I felt like those people on television describing their near-death experience. As I listened to Marsha and Laura's words, pretending to be interested, most of my consciousness was hovering over my disgraceful body pleading with God to open up the earth and swallow me.

"Please, please Lord," I thought, "don't let them ask me where I went to college!" You see friends, I didn't go to college. I got married fresh out of high school and Paul and I got busy starting a family. Though twice accepted to a fine university, I never showed up for class. I'd never regretted that decision either - at least not until that very moment, standing there feeling like a dilapidated shack between two glorious palaces. The waves of insecurity were getting bigger.

What happened next, undoubtedly, was a result of the insecurity rolling around inside of me with so much force that when it found an opening in my body, it seized the opportunity for an escape. I say this because, as I stood before my peers trying to dodge an uncomfortable question, a sudden sound pierced through my body. This sound, which came from an area below my hips and above my knees, is something I don't usually share with the general public. Yes, that's right—the dilapidated shack suddenly became an outhouse—**I tooted**.

Can you believe it? I tooted! I tooted right there in front of Martha Stewart and Cindy Crawford! I could have died; in fact I was hoping that I would. At that moment, I could not have felt more insignificant or vulnerable. Here were my friends, distinguished college graduates, and I, just a measly tooter.

As I stood there, guilty and ashamed by my mailbox, I realized I had some choices to make. I will attempt to write these in an orderly fashion so you can tear them out and keep them in your pocket, in case you find yourself in a similar situation someday.

These are the choices I faced as I clung to my offensive bibs for security:

Step One: **Judge the Sound**. I immediately replayed, in my head, the sound of my toot in order to know my next move. *Did they even hear it?* I wondered. Marsha never even broke her talking stride as she continued about her various college degrees. *That was a good break!* I thought, and I felt my first glimmer of real hope since first greeting Marsha that day. However, during "play back" I realized that at the exact moment of flatulence, "Lovely Laura" did one of those swooping head-turns towards me, her eyes in wide amazement. *Rats! I'm busted!* Laura was my one and only ear-witness. She would be the one I'd have to deal with. Thus, leading me hastily to step two.

Step Two: **Place the Blame Elsewhere—and Hurry**! I decided the way to cover up my little toot was to pull the old, *"I scraped my shoe on the pavement"* ploy. Again, a glimmer of hope crossed my broken spirit. But as I looked down for pavement and shoes my hope was dashed—I was barefoot in the grass. Foiled again!

For a brief moment I considered placing the blame on Marsha, who by the way, was still talking about colleges. I thought about glancing over at Laura and rolling my eyes in disgust towards Marsha.

I decided, however, that that would be too mean-spirited. Besides "Lovely Laura" would never even believe it. Something tells me that if "Clean Marsha" ever does toot, it probably comes out in a tune like one of those fancy doorbells at rich people's homes. While my toot was a monotone gust, hers undoubtedly is a whimsical melody that makes everyone feel welcome and refreshed. Not only that, but I'm willing to bet my dirty bibs that Marsha's toot would smell like hot apple pie. I was forced to proceed to step three.

Step Three: Evacuate! Yes, that's right. I took the coward's way out. Clutching one of my overall straps for moral support, I simply said, "Hey ladies, I'm going to go in and see Paul now." They said, "Goodbye," and Marsha continued to tell Laura about her degrees as I slowly moved my shameful, unrestrained body up the hill. I tried to move gracefully so I wouldn't disturb the air as I trudged toward my house, feeling like a loser. I opened the door and went inside thinking how fortunate it is that I like it in here, seeing that I might never be able to leave it again.

Inside my living room, I crumpled into a big, pitiful heap on the floor. I cried out to God, "Please Lord! Just take me home." I couldn't believe that only ten minutes before I had thought of myself as a rather decent, worthwhile woman. Now, I lay on my carpet as a shabbily dressed, uneducated girl who can't even control her own bodily functions. I looked towards the sky and said, **"Lord, I know Your Word tells us to make a joyful noise, but I don't think this is what You had in mind!"** What a mess.

That day, as I lay on my orange carpet, the Lord quietly reminded me of something. He reminded me that I was the same person right then - as a convicted tooter - as I was before the situation. He helped me realize that my worth wasn't found in the condition of my home, the value of my clothes, or the education I've received. Eventually, as He consoled me, I heard something else come out of my musical body—a giggle, a tee-hee, a laugh! Not only me, I think God was giggling with me.

I wish I could hold that day in front of my mailbox with those wonderful ladies as the single example in my life where I was fooled into thinking my value as a person was tied to temporary things; unfortunately it is only one of many. In the last chapter we looked at the danger of losing our identity in the entanglements of temporary stations. **We can't define ourselves, as people who were made for eternal purposes, by temporary things.** How do we avoid that? We avoid it by making the conscious decision to spend time daily with our eternal Father; He is the only one who can give us eternal definition.

Unfortunately, stations and seasons are not the

only temporary places we can get suckered into placing our self-esteem in. Most women, myself included, habitually struggle with self worth and fall into the trap of assessing their personal value by comparing themselves to others around them. The day I stood in front of my mailbox with Laura and Marsha, I didn't do well in the comparison. That experience left me feeling dried up in my self-esteem reserve.

Because self-esteem issues are so important in the lives of women, I'd like to dive a little deeper into the subject of temporary places we attempt to draw self-worth from. When our self-esteem suffers, other areas in our lives suffer, including our relationship with the Lord. So strap on your diving gear and let's jump in. By the way, if during our dive your ears start to pop, try chewing gum.

Go back to the beginning of this chapter and reread Isaiah 58:11. In my home "a sun-scorched land" is the perfect word picture for many of my days. My long, wide desert is often littered with whining children and toys. Living in that hot land can often drain every drop of moisture within me. Add a longing for romance and a need for affirmation and, presto! I've got myself a dry parched heart. You know what? It's hard to be an effective mommy, wife, friend, sister, or Christian when you've got a dry, parched heart.

When our bodies are dehydrated, we naturally

long for water to refresh us. Keeping that in mind, it only makes sense that when we are dehydrated spiritually and emotionally we long for refreshment in those areas as well.

God's ideal plan is that we come to Him when we are feeling depleted in our body or spirit, so that He can "satisfy our needs and strengthen our frame." In fact, this verse says that God promises to refresh us so that we "will be like a well-watered garden, like a spring whose waters never fail!" When we come to the Lord who offers us eternal refreshment, He is faithful to refresh us abundantly. Isn't that wonderful? **Isn't that why we *always* go to Him when we're thirsty**? Wait . . . *do we* always go to Him?

I don't. You probably don't either. We may look to friends to compliment us, shopping to distract us, or addictions to nurture us, instead of simply giving our needs to the Lord. While other things may give us a temporary feeling of satisfaction or refreshment, the feeling won't last because it came from a temporary source.

Looking to temporary sources for refreshment is not only a losing battle, but it can also be dangerous. If we're looking for flattery to refresh us, we just might find it in a man (whether in person or over the internet) who is all too eager to say just what our thirsty soul is longing to hear. This often happens slowly, one sip at a time, until we wake up and find ourselves drowning in an extramarital affair.

Affairs start slow, often out of the thirst of an unmet need or expectation. When we feel that thirst, it is imperative that we go to God to refresh us. It is also wise to be accountable in this area to another Christian **woman.** Don't settle for foolish, temporary refreshment!

Chocolate, pornography, credit cards, binging-purging, alcohol, and French fries all can represent areas we run to when we feel a thirst within us. Perhaps we think it's easier to go to something or someone that we can see and touch for results. I don't know. But I do know that nothing will take care of our spiritual and emotional thirsts with more love, grace, and plentiful refreshment than our faithful Father. Even when we're not sure why we're thirsty or where the need is coming from, He does. "You will be like a well watered garden; like a spring whose waters never fail." It's a promise.

Are you thirsty? Are there needs in your life that aren't being met in the sun-scorched land you live in? Beautiful friend, bring those needs, that thirst, to the only source of living water - God through Jesus Christ. Come every day and refill as many times as you need. *He will never run dry, and you don't have to either.*

Walking with God. . .
with Toliet Paper Stuck to My Shoe

"As a deer pants for streams of water, so my soul pants for you, O God. My soul thirsts for God, for the living God. Where can I go and meet with God?"
Psalm 42:1–2

Eternal Refreshment

Chapter Three Questions

Getting to know you,
getting to know all about you . . .

1. Come on, share your best toot story . . . you *know* you have one!

2. What is your favorite comfortable outfit? How often do you wear it?

3. Write down three things you absolutely love about yourself.

It's time to apply!

*"No one can make you feel inferior
without your permission."
Eleanor Roosevelt*

Paul writes to the church in Corinth this verse from 2 Corinthians 10:12 talking about false teachers who were trying to prove their worth by comparing themselves to others rather than God's standards: "Oh, don't worry; I wouldn't dare say that I am as wonderful as these other men who tell you how important they are! But they are only comparing themselves with each other, and measuring themselves by themselves. What foolishness!"

4. Do you compare yourself to other people? How do you rate?

5. When you are feeling emotionally or spiritually parched, what refreshment do you faithfully head for?

If you've ever had a garden you know how important it is to water it. (Which is why I don't have a garden!) If your garden doesn't receive adequate refreshment it will dry up and die. If you are counting on enjoying the harvest of that garden, I guess you're out of luck.

As mothers, sisters, wives, daughters, employers, Christians, etc. there are people surrounding us that count on us for nourishment. Whether it be love, support, effort, or faithfulness, they are needing a part of our harvest. If we are cracked, dried-up and stressed-out we not only hurt ourselves, but those around us will be neglected of the rich bounty God wants to bring out of your life.

6. Who, in your life, benefits when you are spiritually refreshed?

Who, in your life, benefits when you are spiritually depleted?

7. Today, would you consider yourself a well-watered garden; like a spring whose waters never fail? If not, when was the last time you felt that way?

Journaling Time

*"O God, you are my God; I earnestly search for you. My soul **thirsts** for you; my whole body **longs** for you in this parched and weary land where there is no water."*
Psalms 63:1

What are the things that dry you out? Knowing these, what can you do to avoid drought?

Read John 4:1–15. This poor Samaritan woman, as I am sure I also would have, struggled to replace her *temporary* thinking with Jesus' bold new *eternal* way of thinking. What were some of the excuses, stumbling blocks, or questions this woman kept bringing up?

Do you ever cling to all the reasons it makes sense for you to be dehydrated emotionally, physically, and spiritually - instead of accepting what Jesus is standing there offering you? If you do, why?

Jesus said to the woman at the well, "People soon become thirsty again after drinking this water. But the water I give them takes away thirst altogether. It becomes a perpetual spring within them, giving them eternal life." John 4:13

Melissa Jansen

Spiritual Refreshment does not
depend on our circumstances.

Some of the people who have touched me the most
are those who know that they can experience the
"perpetual spring of life" within them no matter
their circumstances. People who have no reason
to be refreshed, because of their situations, and
yet mysteriously are *overflowing* with spiritual
refreshment. This refreshment runs over the brims of
their own lives and spills into the lives around them.
What a way to live!

*"May the God of hope fill you with all joy and
peace as you trust in him, so that you may overflow
with hope by the power of the Holy Spirit."
Romans 15:13*

Let's Pray . . .

Lord, thank You for never running dry! I can come to You and drink over and over **every day** and You will never run dry. You are abundant and overflowing. I praise You!

Father, today I learned this:

Holy Spirit, remind me this week of these things:

Jesus, our relationship will benefit from these changes because:

Section Two

FALLING IN LOVE, VIAGRA, AND WAL-MART

"My personal mission is to model a life that exhibits **romance, thrills,** and **adventure.** To equip and train women to be all they can be for Christ, in every circumstance, by loving their neighbor as themselves and **never selling short God's awesome power to change the world through them.** I believe God has called every believer to live life to the very fullest by **dreaming dreams, seizing opportunities, and obeying God."** - Joey Mishler

You'll be reading a lot about Joey Mishler. Joey is a best friend, sister-in-law, confidant, accountability partner, supporter, and mentor - all rolled up into one beautiful gal. Together we giggle at *nothing* and chat about *everything*. We're dreamers, Joey and I, and we have spent countless hours laughing and crying (often at the same time) about all we feel God calling us to.

Joey has such an intimate relationship with Christ that it touches people all around her. I've watched her give generously - even when she was in need. I've watched her reach out to people that I would rather pass by. I've watched her close her mouth when I would rather say totally unnecessary things (- is that hard to believe?). I've witnessed her choose to love, forgive, encourage, and inspire. She's **fabulous** and God has used her life to change me, and many others, in countless ways. I love my Joey.

An intimate relationship with God has not only been offered to Joey, or even a handful of Joeys, but to all of us. Our relationship with God isn't meant to be a cold, crusty list of do's and don'ts but a living, breathing love affair. In this next section, we will look at the relationship between us and God. In Chapter Four, we'll look at falling head over heals in love with Him. Chapter Five examines the distinctive relationship God wants with us. And in Chapter Six, we'll gaze at how this love affair causes us to see Him all around us; that's how it is when you're in love, isn't it?

Ahhh, love is in the air! Let's get started!

Chapter Four

LOVE LETTERS

*"How I delight in your
commands! How I love them!"
Psalm 119:47*

I was seventeen when I saw him, the man of my dreams, for the first time. It was early morning and he was sound asleep on my couch. Slowly, I crouched dangerously close over his slumbering body to get a better look. Although he was covered with a blanket, one of his big, muscular arms dangled out . . . it was naked! I looked at its bulk and I thought, *Wow! Now that's an arm!* My eyes surveyed his short blonde hair and his strong jaw line. *Is it too soon to kiss him?* I wondered. Deciding a kiss was premature, I quietly left the room for fear of being caught by this twenty-one-year-old slumbering Adonis. Or, worse yet, being caught by my 42-year-old father!

Why was this man asleep on my couch, you ask? Did my parents open the door to one man in the community at a time for me to survey in the wee hours of the morning? No, this stranger was there because my brother, Chris, and his new bride, Joey, had arranged for him to meet me. They had suckered him in to working as a counselor for a youth camp I was attending (I was one of the youth!). He had arrived late the night before and fallen asleep on our old orange-plaid sofa.

This sofa, just for your information, was never a couch I had liked before this particular moment. My distaste for it wasn't only biased by the bright orange plaid but more so by it's coarse, scratchy fabric. If you lay on this couch and, heaven-forbid, rolled over—you could count on losing at least two layers of skin. It was rather like a big orange loofa. I used to worry that if I fell asleep on one side of my face longer than the other I would be whittled down lopsided. But now, this old couch was clutching a naked-armed hunk-of-a-man and I forgave it immediately for all its abrasive past.

As it turned out, that night on the couch was the first of many nights spent there for that man - it's a wonder he had any skin left on his body! He turned out not only to be a great camp counselor, but an even better match for me! "He," of course, was Paul Jansen and we were married about a year and a half after our camp experience.

While courting, Paul and I carried on a long-distance relationship. I was a high school senior in Decatur, Indiana; Paul was a college senior at Anderson University, about an hour and a half away. Have you ever had a long distance relationship? Do you remember the agony of saying good-bye and having to count the days till you'd see your loved one again? I do! As soon as my Paulie drove away in his little blue Toyota, I would begin my familiar count-down until the next weekend. I couldn't wait to see his face, hold his hands, and kiss his lips. (Maybe next I'll write a steamy romance novel!)

While Paul and I were apart I was either counting the hours or aching to talk to him on the telephone. I wore holes in all my socks sprinting to the phone whenever it rang just hoping for the sound of my Paul's deep, magnificent voice. His voice had the power to shoot chills straight up my spine while simultaneously sending tingles deep down into my toes like a volt of lightning. It was like dating Barry White. Paul's voice still has the power to give me chills, even today, except when he's saying something like: "Honey, how many checks **did you write**!?" "Hey Missy, when exactly will I have clean clothes to wear?" or "Hon, is this stuff chicken or meatloaf?"

Anyway, Paul and I were madly in love and the phone was an excellent substitute for actually seeing each other . . . that is until the bill came at the end of the month. When the day came for my parents to either buy groceries or pay the phone bill, my Dad decided to lay down the law to me. I was allowed to call Paul twice a week for three minutes or less. Every time I called I had to set the stove timer for three minutes. Once the bell rang, I was financially on my own. Since Paul and I were both broke, we quickly adapted to letter writing.

My daily after-school ritual became sprinting to my mailbox hoping to find a letter addressed to me in the familiar handwriting of my beloved football star! If I was lucky enough to find one I'd throw the rest of the mail back into the box and shoot across my yard with my treasure in hand. I'd race to my bedroom like a great Olympian. Without breaking stride I'd swing my door shut and leap toward my bed covered in a blue butterfly bedspread so slippery that if I dove on just the right spot at the foot of my bed, I could slide clear to the top at a neck-breaking speed. I wasn't very athletic so this was a great thrill for me to achieve. I really feel I could have lettered in it.

As I flew across my bed with letter in hand, I let out a squeal that any lovesick teenage girl would recognize: "EEEEEEEEE!" If you have a hard time imagining the sound, inflate a balloon to its maximum capacity and then pull its mouth tight, letting the air slowly escape. That high-pitched, obnoxious "shriek" is how I would sound while gliding across my bedspread anticipating what I was about to read. *"EEEEEEEEEE!"*

I don't want to brag but my Paul's letters were brilliant! He almost always began them, "Honey . . ." How did he come up with such great stuff? Just the opening was enough to make me clutch the letter to my chest and send more teenage balloon noises up to the Heavens. I'd get hot behind my ears as I giggled, "He called me, Honey!" Slowly, as I squealed my way through the letter I would read glorious things like:

"I love you!" "I think about you all the time!"
"Someday we will be together forever!"

Oh, I just loved it! At the end of the letter I would smile and sigh - completely satisfied like after a Thanksgiving dinner - as I carefully put the letter back into its envelope and into a drawer specifically designated for such fortune. I loved my Paulie. I loved his letters. I loved my balloon noises

Fast forward to about five years ago. Paul and I were married with three little kiddies and we had just moved into the house in which I'm now sitting. One day, while in our new attic, I discovered a little brown cardboard box left by the previous owner. Now, I knew it wasn't ours and, though I studied it with great curiosity, **I knew it would have been in bad taste to open it!**

When I opened the box I discovered it was full of what looked like high school notes - the ones you fold into little squares and pass to each other between classes. Although I looked at the folded letters with great curiosity, **I knew it would have been in bad taste to read someone else's letters!**

When I read the letters I deduced that they must have been sent to a teenage boy that lived in our house twenty years before. He'd apparently had quite an admirer. I only read a couple of the messages, but the basic ideas expressed were these:

"I love you!" "I think about you all the time!" "Someday we will be together forever!"

Putting the letters down, I said out loud, "Oh Brother! What a bunch of bologna!" I took the whole box and put it somewhere safe, where no nibby-nose person would be able to read them. (Smile!)

As soon as the box hit the garbage can I had a flashback of a balloon-squealing girl, sliding across her butterfly bedspread. *Hmmm . . . curious,* I thought. When Paul wrote the same words they made me swoon and giggle. Now reading those words, written by someone else's hand made me want to scoff and gag. What was the difference?

It's simple, really. The difference was *my love for the author.*

You see, I loved Paul's letters because I loved Paul. **It wasn't so much the words that made me love Paul; it was Paul that made me love the words.**

Around this same time, I was leading a group of women through a book study of the Psalms. All along I was really dreading the fated day that we would have to study Psalm 119. This particular Psalm is an acrostic poem set to the Hebrew alphabet and, if you don't already know, is incredibly long . . . almost five pages in length - and the Bible uses such tiny type!

Will my group of ladies take the time to read all this at home? I worried to myself as I sat down to do my study. *How will we fit all the discussion into our short time together?* I couldn't help but inwardly wish that the author of this study would have skipped 119 all together. However, as I reluctantly began to dive-in to this beautiful Psalm the Holy Spirit began to speak to me through this scripture in an entirely new way. Isn't the Lord always faithful to show us new things to apply to our lives?

This time as I read Psalm 119, I was blown away at the beautiful love affair between the Psalmist and God. The words describing the writer's love and respect for scripture were like a banquet of exquisite foods that I have never tasted. The depth of this love was like a world I had never explored. I suddenly felt like I was missing out on so much. Taste and explore some of these verses with me.

> Psalms 119:20, *"My soul is **consumed with longing** for your laws at all times."*

> Verse 103, *"How sweet are your words to my taste, **sweeter than honey to my mouth!**"*

> Verse 111, *"Your statutes are my heritage forever; **they are the joy of my heart**."*

> Verse 148, *"My eyes stay open through the watches of the night, that I may **meditate** on your promises."*

> Verse 174 & 175, *"**I long for your salvation**, O Lord, and your law is my delight. Let me live that I may praise you, and may your laws sustain me."*

On and on the Psalmist goes about his great

longing and love for God's laws and for the scriptures, or the letters God ordained. As I read these passionate verses my heart turned inward. Why, I thought, don't I feel this way about scripture? I have even more of it than this Psalmist did in his day and I don't lay awake through the night thinking about it. What's the difference?

It's simple, really. The difference was **my love for the author**.

The psalmist loved God greatly and knew God so intimately that when he read Scripture it wasn't a one-dimensional arrangement of words meant for someone else - like the letters I found in my attic. No, out of his deep relationship with God, the Bible became a living, breathing love letter from his best friend. Just as Paul's letters to me were not some separate entity, scripture and God are one and the same. The Psalmist feasted on God's words with a passionate appetite that I covet. I want to love God's scripture like that. Even more, I want to love God like that.

Corrie ten Boom lived with passionate love for God and His word. *The Hiding Place*, is Corrie's book describing her experiences up to, and during, her family's imprisonment in Nazi concentration camps. I've read this book several times and am always pierced by the beauty shown by Corrie and her sister, Betsy, in spite of their hellish situation. How could these two frail women, in the midst of thick, consuming death, be so committed to witness about Life?

The source of this Life, of course, was their relationship with Jesus Christ. It was rekindled day after day reading from their little, smuggled Bible. Corrie and Betsy depended on the truth they found between the crumpled covers of God's word to survive. Let me share this excerpt from Corrie as she endured a concentration camp called Ravensbrook:

"Sometimes I would slip the Bible from its little sack with hands that shook, so mysterious had it (scripture) become to me. It was new: it had just been written. *I marveled sometimes that the ink was dry.* I had believed the Bible always, but reading it now had nothing to do with belief. It was simply a description of the way things were - of hell and heaven, of how men act and how God acts. I had read a thousand times the story of Jesus' arrest - how soldiers had slapped Him, laughed at Him, flogged Him. Now such happenings had faces and voices."

Corrie's life in Ravensbrook is a generous illustration of how scripture is alive. We can see how it rose up off the printed page and became a living, breathing source of hope to a crowded mass of beaten, hungry women lying on lice covered mats each night under a single light bulb. The Bible wasn't a casual option to read whenever they got a spare minute. It wasn't a collection of words that seemed foreign and out-dated. The Word became a survival necessity just as much as food and water. Its words were to them, fresh from the very lips of their God, that very day—that very moment.

I feel certain that as Corrie or Betsy took that worn book from its hiding place each night and began to whisper the words of hope, forgiveness, and love to the huddled women surrounding them, that in their hearts they were squealing with delight to hear the words from their Beloved:

"I love you." I think about you all the time."
"Someday we will be together forever."

Corrie and Betsy - like the Psalmist, had such a tremendous love for the **Author of Life** that they fell desperately in love with His words, commands, and will. I ache to get to the point where I daily dive across my bedspread with my letters from God and read, with hunger and excitement, all He has to tell me. I long to recognize His handwriting as I touch the ink to see if it's dry.

God Loves You

*"And I pray that Christ will be more and more at home in your hearts as you trust in him. May your roots go down deep into **the soil of God's marvelous love**. And may you*

*have the power to understand, as all God's people should, **how wide, how long, how high, and how deep his love really is.** May you experience the love of Christ, though it is so great you will never fully understand it. Then you will be filled with the fullness of life and power that comes from God."*
Ephesians 3:17–19

God Thinks About You All the Time!

*"How precious are your thoughts about me, O God! **They are innumerable!** I can't even count them; they outnumber the grains of sand! And when I wake up in the morning, you are still with me!"*
Psalms 139:17–18
(Read the whole chapter!)

Someday You Can Be With God Forever!

*"I am the resurrection and the life. Those who **believe in me**, even though they die like everyone else, **will live again."***
John 11:25

Squeal it with me ladies. . . EEEEEEEEEE!

Love Letters

Chapter Four Questions

Getting to know you,
getting to know all about you . . .

1. Who was your first crush? What did you like about him?

2. Did anybody ever read a love letter you wrote that wasn't supposed to? How did that make you feel?

3. Have you ever read a love letter that was not your own?

It's time to apply!

The difference was my love for the author.

4a. Do you have a verse in the Bible that means a lot to you? If you do, write it down and tell why it is so special to you.

4b. What's that? You say you can't think of a favorite verse right now? That's all right! We've been talking about the book of Psalms this lesson and it's a great place to find meaningful, life-applicable verses. Here are some more great Psalms—claim one, (or two or three), for yourself! Select one, write it out, and tell why it is special to you.

Psalm 4:8 Psalm 37:5 Psalm 92:4 Psalm 139:17–18

Psalm 18:1–2 Psalm 59:16 Psalm 71:15 Psalm 143:8, 10–11

5. Do you think your attitude toward reading the Bible faithfully, whether good or bad, is a reflection of your love for the Author? Why?

Quiet time, devotions, prayer time—these are words we use to describe a set amount of time we sit and focus on God. I believe a discipline of sitting down and focusing on our Heavenly Father is vital and you will find me speaking about this importance throughout this book. However, we are God's girls twenty-four hours a day, not just when we sit down and declare it "time with God."

Likewise, I am Paul Jansen's wife all day long because of a commitment I made to him. I am continuing to learn how that commitment needs to be obvious in the way I dress, the way I speak, the way I greet other men, the decisions I make, and the conversations I have. That's a big commitment! How healthy would my marriage be if I acted married to Paul for a short period of the day but lived the rest of my day however I wanted? No matter how great that short period of my day went, the rest of my day would tell the real story.

6. Can you tell a difference in your life when you are taking time to focus on God's word? What is the difference?

7. What are some changes you need to make in your daily living that would make it more obvious that you have a 24 hour commitment, a love affair, with God?

Journaling Time

Let's have a little fun! Think about a characteristic of God that you have experienced. It could be that you understand His kindness because you have known the gentleness of His hand. Possibly you understand His patience because of His endurance in pursuing you. Whatever the characteristic is, take a few minutes and consider how that characteristic has affected your relationship with Him.

Now, it's time to write! Take that characteristic you thought of and write a love letter to God. You can add as many different characteristics as you want in your love letter. Be careful not to be too general. For instance, what means more to you: "You look nice today," or "You look so pretty in that color! It really shows off your beautiful eyes"? I'd take either, but I love to be complimented specifically. To me, details show intentional thought and focus.

Keep in mind there are countless ways we have each experienced our God - there are no wrong letters. It doesn't matter how simple or how brilliant it turns out. God will love it! But then again, who doesn't love getting a love letter?!

Do you think God makes balloon noises?

Dear God,

Let's Pray . . .

Lord, Thank You for loving me, thinking about me, and making a way for me to be with You forever. You are the ultimate Lover of my Soul.

Read your love letter to the Lord.

Father, today I learned this:

Holy Spirit, remind me this week of these things:

Jesus, our relationship will benefit from these changes because:

Chapter Five

VICARIOUS LIVING

"I will give them a heart to know me,
that I am the Lord."
Jeremiah 24:7

When my nephew, Silas, was about seven years old he came down the stairs of his home one day and announced to his mother, Joey, that he had just been talking to Jesus.

"You have?" Joey asked. "What did you talk about?"

Silas casually answered, "Oh, I just asked Him some questions."

"Like what?" inquired Joey, not knowing how serious she should take this.

"Like . . . like I asked Him, when He was a kid, if anybody ever picked on Him?" (Silas was living through this experience himself, at the moment.)

"And what did Jesus say?" said a now very interested mother.

"He told me there was this one boy who kind of gave Him some trouble." Silas continued, "So I asked Him if He ever felt like beating the boy up. Jesus said that He felt like it, but never did."

Joey put down her dishrag and said, "What else did you talk about?"

"Hmmm, I asked Him if He ever wrestled with His dad, and . . . Oh, I was looking at my little picture of Him while I was talking so I asked Him if this is really what He looked like. Jesus said, 'Not really. My beard is thicker and I'm better looking!' "

Joey believes, as I do, that this was a real experience with the Lord. Can't you just see Jesus relating to a child in such a simple way? It was a time of faith building for Sy, not to mention the rest of the family. What a personal friend Jesus is!

I told Sy's story to my children. As I was relaying the questions and answers to them, I noticed six-year-old Adam was particularly intrigued. His eyes grew glossy and his mouth slowly dropped open in wonder. Not long after I finished, Adam approached me in his "all-business" attitude and said, "Mom, I'm going to go up to my room now and talk to Jesus."

Adam turned toward the stairs and climbed with a determined stride up to his room. I'm certain he was already practicing how to put into words the beautiful experience he was about to embark on.

Watching Adam climb those stairs set my panic alarm off. *What would happen to his little heart if the Lord doesn't speak to him?* As soon as his sweet feet hit the steps I began to pray, "Oh, please Lord, don't let his faith be hindered in any way." I returned nervously to the kitchen where I busied myself until I eventually forgot about my six-year-old's indomitable soul-journey upstairs.

I'm not sure exactly how much time had passed when I heard Adam's little voice behind me. With the same grin he uses while hiding a frog in his pocket, he said, "Hey Mom. Jesus talked to me."

Staring into his charming face, my brain and heart began wrestling each other for the right response. My brain didn't want to make hearing from Jesus sound like an event we can conjure up whenever we have a spare minute, and yet, my heart didn't want to belittle Adam's sweet faith. Warily, my lips settled for the rather wimpy response, "Oh, He did?"

Adam came back proudly, "Yep! You want to know what He said?"

"Sure," I answered, holding my breath.

"Well, I was holding my Bible and I asked Him if everything in here is true."

Drawing in one long lungful of air I said, "And what did He say?"

My fair-haired, eager boy replied matter-of-factly, "Jesus said, 'No.'"

My brain and heart quit wrestling and simply went numb. Smiling, I took Adam's little hands and talked with him about biblically recognizing the voice of our Lord. We talked of how we can be like a flock of sheep who will only come to the familiar call of their shepherd (John 10:2–4). We talked about how sometimes we have to discern Jesus' voice from other voices (John 10:5), and how one way to test if we are hearing God's voice is to make sure it's in harmony with the Bible and God's Spirit (1 John 4:1–4). We talked about the holiness of scripture and how 2 Timothy 3:16 promises that "All scripture is God breathed."

Finally I said, "Adam, I think maybe what you heard doesn't match up with those verses, do you?"

Adam cocked his head and said, "No," while

giving me the "frog-in-my-pocket" smile again. Then he started to re-adjust his story a little bit.

"Oh, yeah! Now I remember. Jesus said that *all* scripture *is* true, but just some of the words aren't spelled right."

My son and I talked further about how learning to recognize the Good Shepherd's voice takes time. I assured him that he didn't have to have the same kind of experience that Silas had talked about. "God is unique, Bubby, and so are His plans for you. Your relationship with Him will be one-of-a-kind."

Before I dismiss this kind of mimicking as behavior confined to children, let me share a little spiritual impersonation of my own. While I was in high school I had a wonderful friend named Aleta McAhren who was in college. I loved Aleta and admired her relationship with the Lord very much. So much so, that when she told me about some special experiences she'd shared with God, I was all ears.

"I go into my dorm room and shut the door," narrated Aleta. "I lay on my back with my knees up, and I put my Bible on my chest." Extending her arms over her head she continued, "Then I raise my hands in the air, try to only focus on God, and I sing to Him and pray."

Without a doubt, as Aleta described the details of her precious experiences, my eyes grew glossy and my mouth slowly dropped open with wonder. (It's a heredity response, I think.) Aleta's encounter sounded awesome! It seemed so easy, so foolproof. This was exactly the experience with God I was looking for. I couldn't wait to get home and have a special time with God—Aleta style!

As soon as I got home I ran to my bedroom, shut the door, lay down on the floor, and put my knees up. Opening my Bible I laid it neatly across my chest and raised my hands towards the ceiling. Hot Dog! I was already feeling more spiritual.

With my body in the endorsed position I started to pray. I prayed about everything I could think of and tried to use big, impressive words whenever possible. Next I belted out some old classic hymns. When I couldn't remember all the words I'd simply make new ones up. I was the "Weird Al Yankovich" of church mantras.

After completing every hymn I could think of, since nothing spiritual seemed to be happening, I decided I should pray again - then sing again. Pray . . . sing . . . pray . . . sing - *the blessings ought to start pouring down on me any minute now,* I thought. Pray . . . sing . . . pray - my arms were starting to go numb. Pray . . . sing . . . pray - boredom was setting in. I was having a hard time concentrating on only God. I started wondering what Mom would be cooking for dinner . . . pray . . . sing—Hey, how long has that cobweb been on my ceiling? Focus now . . . pray . . . sing . . . **STOP!**

Horror gripped me! What if my two brothers had quietly opened my door and were watching me? Red faced, I turned to look. Whew, no brothers. I got up and locked the door. Oh rats, I broke my stride! Where was I? Would I have to begin the whole thing over?

Other doubts began to plague my thoughts. I wondered if I had the Bible open to the right page and if, perhaps, it was sing-then pray, instead of pray-then sing. *Oh, why didn't I have Aleta write this all down?*

When my throat was too sore to re-sing another hymn and my deadened arms were drained of blood, I finally gave up. Feeling very foolish and unsettled I accused myself of reasons why the Lord hadn't ministered to me the way He did to Aleta. *What was wrong with me?*

Nearly twenty years later, I now realize what I was doing wrong that day while trying to mimic Aleta. *I was chasing an experience rather than seeking an intimate God.* I was putting my faith in a technique, not a relationship.

Ladies, I don't share these stories to be flippant. I haven't any doubt Aleta's experience with the Lord was precious and real and I wholeheartedly believe Jesus spoke to Silas. I share these stories to illustrate the truth that we cannot take someone else's encounter with God and adopt them as a surefire recipe for spiritual bliss. In other words, *we cannot live vicariously through someone else's experiences with the Lord.*

Vicariously. That's such a funny word. When I try to use the word *"vicariously"* in a sentence, it usually comes out *"viagrally."* Imagine my embarrassment as I face a crowd of people and proclaim, "We cannot live *viagrally* through someone else's experiences with the Lord." Although we could all use a little extra oompff in our relationship with the Lord, there are other ways to do that - without a prescription.

"Vicarious" simply means "to substitute." Sadly, many people approach their spiritual life by attempting to substitute someone else's experience for their own. As I did with Aleta, and Adam did with Silas, we try to mimic another person's experience. We settle for a spiritual quick-fix.

The Quick-Fix Approach

My husband obnoxiously spews the only true formula for losing weight to me every time I have a new diet idea. He'll say, "Eat less, exercise more, Babe."

"Thanks Sweetie!" I say with a smile knowing what I really meant was, "Shut-up Paul." Then I close my eyes and pray for God to pack about forty pounds on him, just for a week or so.

You see, the truth that Paul has faithfully embraced, "Eat less, exercise more," is not a truth I'm exactly fond of because exercise makes me all sweaty and cheesecake **just so happens** to be my soul mate. I would much rather take a "New Improved" weight loss pill, or drink a "Never Fail" shake. However, I admit that until I decide to put forth the effort and work toward the truth, my body will not look its best. (Don't tell Paul I just said that.)

The quick-fix method doesn't work in developing an authentic, intimate relationship with God either, although it would be nice if it did. Wouldn't it be great to come to God with thirty pounds of bad habits, stubborn behaviors, and selfish tendencies and watch them simply fall off by taking a pill or placing a Bible on our chest? Imagine, "Instant Spiritual Maturity" without all the years of discipline and obedience. The ironic problem with this scenario is that true maturity often comes through the things we'd like to skip - the discipline and obedience. Until we make the decision to experience God ourselves, our relationship with Him will not be its best.

In our last chapter we talked about falling in love with God. It's obvious that if we don't spend time with our Lord we can't really know Him intimately. If you need help organizing your prayer time or guidance in building a relationship with God, please talk to a seasoned Christian woman. Listen to her advice, incorporate fresh ideas, new devotionals, pretty journals, and other creative, godly ideas. Remember though, ***the secret to a rich relationship with God isn't found in the technique you use. It's found in faithfully, obediently coming to Him with a humble, hungry heart***.

Don't be fooled into chasing a technique or an experience - chase God. Actually, He's chasing you. You just need to consistently place yourself where you can be caught.

When we try quick fixes - we miss out.

The Vulture Approach

Some people also miss out by taking what I call the "vulture" approach. These individuals aren't even willing to make the effort to mimic someone else. At least those who mimic desire a better experience with God enough to **do** something. Spiritual vultures don't even make an attempt to nourish their relationship with Christ. They are quite content to live off of other people's Christian experience. They settle for being scavengers like the big birds we see lazily circling in the sky in search of their next easy meal. Unfortunately scores of spiritual vultures fill church pews each Sunday morning.

When your Pastor preaches, the sermons are meant to edify the body of Christ and feed your soul. No matter how meaty those words are, however, they are not meant to be your spiritual breakfast, lunch, dinner, and midnight snack. To really know what God is doing in our lives, and what He is calling us to do, we must spend time growing close to Him. Individually, we need to invest time getting to know His gentle voice, His beautiful heart, and His perfect will.

Don't misunderstand. As Christians we're called to be a part of a church body and the Lord desires to feed us spiritually while we meet. He wants to feed us as a church and as an individual. However, if the only spiritual food we consume all week is spoon fed to us by one or two people as we sit in a pew, we are spiritual vultures who are in danger of spiritual malnourishment. **Jesus died so we could each know Him personally.**

Don't circle idly, waiting for a pastor, teacher, or friend to toss you some spiritual scraps to devour.

Jesus has so much more for you - a nourishing spiritual banquet. Getting to really know Christ is a wonderful, rewarding adventure meant for each one of us. Here's how the first chapter of 2 Peter describes that adventure:

> "As we know Jesus better, his divine power gives us everything we need for living a godly life. He has called us to receive his own glory and goodness! (vs. 5) So make every effort to apply the benefits of these promises to your life. Then your faith will produce a life of moral excellence. A life of moral excellence leads to knowing God better. Knowing God leads to self-control. Self-control leads to patient endurance, and patient endurance leads to godliness. Godliness leads to love for other Christians, and finally you will grow to have genuine love for everyone. The more you grow like this, the more you will become productive and useful in your knowledge of our lord Jesus Christ." (verses 3, 5–8, NLT).

How about it? Are you living vicariously through someone else's spiritual experience? Are you pursuing a "surefire" technique rather than an authentic, intimate relationship with Christ? Do you suspect you may be a spiritual vulture - just gathering enough scraps off other people's relationship with God to get by?

My friend, God is unique and so are His plans for you. His relationship with you will be one of a kind. Don't settle for living vicariously. Don't settle for living "viagrally" either.

Vicarious Living

Chapter Five Questions

Getting to know you, getting to know all about you . . .

1. If you could ask Jesus one question, what would it be?

2. Who do you consider to be the most famous person you've ever spoken to?

3. Thinking of yourself as a cook, which of these three women is the most like you:

a) "My favorite way of cooking is grabbing a frozen dinner, already prepared for me, and throwing it in an oven. It's quick, convenient, and best yet, if it doesn't turn out it's not my fault! *To me, cooking dinner is just a chore to check off my list for the day.*"

b) "My favorite way of cooking is using recipes that I have already tested and know that they work. I don't have a lot of variety, but many of my recipes are from family and friends - they are tried and true - and I like them. *To me, cooking dinner should be comfortable and familiar.*"

c) "I like variety. I like to try new recipes, seasonings, and techniques. Because I get bored easily, I enjoy thumbing through magazines for new and interesting cooking ideas. *To me, cooking dinner is a creative way of expressing myself.*"

It's time to apply!

"My heart has heard you say, "Come and talk with me." And my heart responds, "Lord, I am coming."
Psalm 27:8*

4. Look at your answer for your cooking type in question #3. There are numerous factors that could have affected your answer: schedules, confidence, how many people depend on you, etc. Do those same factors flavor your approach to your prayer time? How so?

I was chasing an experience
rather than seeking an intimate God.

I was putting faith in a technique,
not a relationship.

5. Have you ever tried putting your faith in a technique to experience God? How did that work for you?

Let me give you a little background on this next verse. Paul was zealous to free people from the restraints of the law (Old Testament) by teaching them the freedom of grace found only in Jesus Christ (New Testament). He fervently taught people, Jew and Gentile, that a relationship with God no longer depended on heritage, rituals, or traditions. Imagine Paul's frustration to find out, after watching new Christians experience this exciting new freedom, that they had been convinced to place the old restraints of the law back on.

Read the words that Paul said to the Church of Corinth in 1Corinthians 4:14–16.

6. We've been talking about how we shouldn't mimic other people's experiences to encounter God. Did this passage shoot down all we've just talked about? If not, what's the difference?

7. Do you have a spiritual mentor?

8. A spiritual vulture is **someone who survives spiritually, solely off of other people's experiences with God.** What is the danger of living this way?

<u>Journaling Time</u>

I have three children and love them each the same, but that doesn't mean I have a carbon-copy relationship with each of them. One example of the differences in our relationships would be in the way they enjoy an intimate moment with me. For example, Adam loves it when I listen to his wild stories or dreams for the future. Ryan absolutely loves a quiet time of being held and cuddled, while Madison enjoys going on walks alone with me. I enjoy the differences in my kids because it adds to the distinctness of our relationships. I'll bet you can see that in your family as well.

If we, as human parents, enjoy the intimacy of our children's uniqueness, don't you think our Heavenly Father enjoys a distinct relationship with each of us as well?

Melissa Jansen

What is a distinct quality you know in your relationship
with God?

Write out Psalm 116:1–2

Let's Pray . . .

Lord, thank You for the intimate, personal, distinct relationship You desire to have with me. It blows me away to know that You, the King of the Universe, are happy to see me quiet myself before You every day! You are such an incredible Father to me!

Father, today I learned this:

Holy Spirit, remind me this week of these things:

Jesus, our relationship will benefit from these changes because:

Chapter Six

SPIRITUAL SENSES

"But blessed are your eyes, because they see; and your ears because they hear."
Matthew 13:16

When we enter into our own loving, intimate relationship with God - like we've been talking about so far in this section, the Holy Spirit opens our eyes to His working all around us. We begin to recognize our day as arranged by a precious God rather than cheap coincidence. Being intimate with the Author of Life awakens our spiritual senses, allowing us to *really* see, *really* hear, *really* live for the Kingdom's purpose.

Let me share an experience when the Holy Spirit opened my spiritual senses. During the Christmas rush, in the middle of Wal-Mart, I observed God's love, His excitement, and His longing for one of His lost children.

Our van desperately needed new tires for some holiday traveling and I was more than happy to volunteer for the task. I arrived at Wal-Mart in style, wearing my new black suede coat and matching scarf. Of all the lovely gifts I'd generously bought for myself this Christmas season, my coat and scarf were the definite favorites. Feeling quite charming, wrapped in suede, I walked into the auto center.

"How long will it take to get new tires for my van?" I asked the clerk in the wrinkled blue vest. She looked at my coat and scarf and coveted them in her heart (I'm able to sense these things). "Oh, it'll be *at least* and hour and a half, maybe even two hours, before we can look at it," she said, staring at my scarf. "Then it'll take another forty-five minutes just to put the tires on." She and I both knew I could cut my time in half by simply sliding my scarf across the counter to her, but I wasn't interested. Because of the snow, my kids had been home every day for the past week and now they were officially off for two more weeks of Christmas vacation. Believe me, a two and a half hour wait in Wal-Mart sounded like a day at the spa. I'll keep my scarf.

Being snow-bound in the house with children is kind of like a dog's age. Every year for a dog is actually like seven. Every day trapped in the house with three sugared-up kids is, emotionally speaking, actually like seven. So if you add my kids' snow days to their Christmas break, by the time I send them off on that gorgeous yellow bus again, it will have seemed like they were home for 147 days straight! That's inhumane.

Snow days start off fun and exciting. The kids and I congregate in my bed and curl up under the covers to protect ourselves from the dark, cold, winter morning. We giggle and listen to the wonderful, God-fearing radio man. "Hush now my darlings." I say with love and a twinkle in my eye. "Here come the school closings."

"Anderson Community schools are canceled," proclaims our beloved disc jockey. The kids and I scream in triumph and plan out our day while nestled in the house together.

"Let's bake cookies!" "Let's play games!" "Let's read books!"

Yeah well, after a couple of days of this "togetherness," I lay alone in my bed, cold and bitter. In the wee hours of the morning I listen to the vile radioman's voice-of-doom. Deep wrinkles are embedded in my forehead and my eyes have adopted a nervous twitch. With thick, crusty breath I warn the radio-twerp that if he dares to call off school today, my hooligans are joining him at the station!

You see, snow isn't fun anymore. Hot cocoa makes me want to puke, and my children are now fighting over such things as, "Who has the bigger face?" And, "Who can run through the kitchen faster without using their legs?" What they don't realize is, if we have much more of this stinking "togetherness," they'll be lucky to even *have* legs.

That is why, as I stood before the Wal-Mart tire clerk and received my two and a half hour sentence, I was able to smile and say that the wait would be fine. I took a cart and set out for some alone time with my well-dressed self.

I took three long, leisurely laps around the store. It was getting hot and I was sweating clear through my suede. However, taking off my coat wasn't an option because I was wearing an old, stained T-shirt under it. My stylishness is very shallow. Bored and uncomfortable, I suddenly felt compelled to pick a fight with some other mommy by saying, "Hey! I bet my face is bigger than yours!" Instead, I decided to get a bite to eat in the little deli. Thank goodness.

I stood in line and pilfered through my pocketbook like an archeologist digging for bones. People behind me were getting restless as my fingers raked through the cookie crumbs and dirty Tic Tacs crusted to the bottom of my purse. Trying to promote peace, I offered each of them a hairy Tic Tac, but there were no takers. A disappointing $2.37 was all I could unearth.

The BLT for $1.78 sounded like the right choice. I really wanted the onion rings too, but they were an additional $1.89 and my fingers were too sore to dig any farther down in my purse. A saggy-faced lady took my order. She looked like she had been snowbound in the house with her kids for far too many snow days. I shined-up a Tic Tac on my coat sleeve and offered it to her. Still, no takers.

So, there I sat in the middle of Wal-Mart's snack bar eating my BT sandwich ("Saggy-face" forgot the lettuce). I took my time eating. This was easy because my bacon was a little extra chewy and my mouth was confused with whether to swallow it or blow a bubble. Gnawing on my last bite, I looked at the clock on the wall. Can you imagine my horror when I realized it had only been twenty-five minutes since I first arrived? The only thing left to do was sit and watch the people walking by. That, and scrape the wads of bacon off the bottom of the table.

My eyes landed on a young daddy holding his infant son. All my frustrations melted away as this father kissed his son's wee cheeks and bounced him in a gentle rhythm usually reserved for a mother's arms. A deep feeling of thanksgiving unexpectedly poured over me as I remembered the amazement of the Christmas season. It all began with the love between a Father and his Son! I closed my eyes and thanked God for being willing to let go of His only Child, so that I might know salvation. What a tender, merciful Father He is. Watching the daddy in front of me continue to cuddle his baby into his chest, I knew my eyes were witnessing how my God longs to hold me . . . how He longs to hold that father . . . how He longs to hold that sweet baby.

> *"He (God) tends his flock like a shepherd:*
> *He gathers the lambs in his arms*
> *and carries them close to his heart;*
> *He gently leads those that have young."*
> *Isaiah 40:11 NIV*

I got up and started to walk around. My mood had completely changed. An excitement grabbed me as I began to intentionally look for God's hand on the people around me. Every time someone passed I became overwhelmed at how my Lord knows and loves each one passionately. I honestly felt as though every person was placed there for me to see as a witness of God's great love. I wasn't experiencing a warm-fuzzy thought, it was a profound awakening to God's desire for all His people and the great plans He has for each of us. My heart pounded at His devotion to that lady pushing her cart full of presents; the man waiting nervously at the cash register; the child whining for candy. The hugeness of God took my breath away! What a privilege to know Him.

Loud voices gathered my attention toward the men's department. Only a moment was needed to know that the two people speaking were mentally challenged. With excited tones they discussed a gift they needed to buy for someone.

"Hey, what color would he like?"

"Ummm, blue . . . this one!"

"No. I, I think the red is better!"

"Red? Are you sure? . . . Okay, yeah! Red **is** better!"

"He will really, really like this, huh?!"

"Oh, Yeah!"

I watched and listened to this couple as though I thought I was invisible. The raw enthusiasm in their voices held me captive. The more they decided how perfect the red shirt was for their loved one, the louder and more excited each became. "Oh! If only I could be there to watch that gift being opened!" I cried to myself, finally able to walk away. The couple's joy of giving was so beautiful and pure that it infectiously spread inside me. I traveled down the isles absolutely brimming with anticipation for the season. I thought, *isn't this just like my Lord?* He gives with joy! Whether it is His love, patience, forgiveness, or even His own Son. He gives with absolute joy.

> *"For God so loved the world that*
> *He gave His one and only Son,*
> *that whoever believes in Him shall not*
> *perish but have eternal life."*
> *John 3:16*

Tired and sweaty, I steered my cart to the auto center. There were two new workers behind the counter but neither cared about, nor acknowledged, my arrival. I sat in a plastic chair while they regaled each other with stories. One gloated about how drunk she planned on getting that night at a Christmas party and her plan of calling in sick the next morning. The other made comments of how the manager would never catch on and they giggled about the whole situation. After a few minutes one girl left for her party, leaving the other woman to fend for herself behind the counter.

The remaining lady wore a "Donna" nametag. She was rather heavy-set and dressed in jeans and a sweatshirt. Her long hair was bushy and I liked the way it hung unevenly in the back. Donna's hard, weathered face mouthed words with no sounds and I studied her as though she were another object lesson God put in my path that night.

Donna caught me off guard when she suddenly looked my way. I smiled. Turning her face away she said with a smuggled giggle in her voice, "I just got in trouble from my manager. Somebody complained to him that I look like I'm always mad at the world."

Surprised at her transparency I said, "Well, Donna, I don't think you look mad at the world."

Strangely proud, Donna responded, "Well, that's what happens when you're manic-depressive".

I said, "Oh, is that what you are?"

"Yes," she grinned.

The phone rang and I prayed that the Lord would give me words to share with Donna. She hung up the phone and resurrected our dead conversation by saying, "Yep, it's just good for me to make it through the day without breaking down in tears. They (Wal-Mart) should be glad I'm at least here."

Like a bathing suit in December, Donna's smile looked totally useless to our conversation as she continued, "This is the first year in the last three or so, that I haven't been hospitalized this close to Christmas. I just hate Christmas! I'm hoping to make it through without going back to the hospital."

I couldn't help but wonder if I was the

fourteenth person to hear this story today or if this was God ordained. I said, "Oh, were you in the hospital because of depression?"

"Oh yeah," she jumped, "either for depression or some different surgeries I've had."

"Donna, Christmas is kind of funny, isn't it?" I said. "It brings so much joy for some - and so much pain for others."

She smiled and smugly responded, "I don't have any joy."

The phone rang again, as if on cue, and Donna went to it. When she returned she told me how she had just moved here from Canada about six months ago with her two kids. We talked about her Christmas plans with her nephew. I was on a secret mission to try to point out all the good she was mentioning, but Donna kept changing it back into the statement; "I don't have any joy."

"Donna, do you and your kids go to church anywhere?" I asked. "I would love for you to come to my church."

Still carrying a slight smirk, she patted her dingy sweatshirt and said, "Oh, this is all I have. I don't wear dresses and stuff."

Suddenly, I wished I were only sitting there wearing my stained T-shirt as I told Donna, unconvincingly, how clothes weren't important at my church. "A sweatshirt and jeans would be just great," I said.

I told Donna briefly about the joy I know in the Lord and that maybe this season she could find some new joys; perhaps she could let go of some of her old pain and find new peace. Donna listened to me, but she would only say, "Well I don't know . . . I don't know."

A couple of customers came and I left to go get some fingernail polish remover. When I got back Donna was shelving air fresheners. We made small talk until my van was finished. When I was about to leave I said, "Donna, I don't think you look mad at the world. I'm going to be praying that you find some new joy this year."

She quietly responded, "Oh, maybe *after* Christmas."

I interrupted her in a teasing way, "Donna, I'm praying for you to find some new joy *before* Christmas."

We laughed and talked a little more and then I left. Donna was all smiles again but as I walked out the door I heard her say to anyone who would listen, "People think I look like I'm mad at the world."

When I finally climbed into my newly-shoed van that night, I felt somewhat like a feather with a big brick on top of it. I felt light and excited about being reminded of God's great love for His people, but at the same time, I felt heavily burdened for those who aren't aware of that love. I wanted so much for Donna to catch a glimpse of that precious gift this Christmas.

I wanted Donna to see how God would love to hold her in His arms, close to His heart—like that daddy and his baby boy. I wanted Donna to see how joyfully God gave us the gift of His Son and eternal life. I wanted her to see that there was more than drunken parties and hopeless holidays available to her. I wanted Donna to unwrap God's gifts to her— gifts of hope, peace, real love, and healing.

> *"You turned my wailing into dancing;*
> *you removed my sackcloth and*
> *clothed me with joy, that my heart may sing*
> *to you and not be silent. O Lord my God,*
> *I will give you thanks forever."*
> *Psalm 30:11–12 NIV*

I'd love to end this story by telling you that I saw Donna at church the next Sunday. It would be a great ending to this chapter to be able to say that Donna now knows Jesus and has found her joy in Him, but I can't. I'm not even sure she made it through the holidays without checking back into the hospital. I do know that I prayed for her. I do know that God is longing for her. I do know that there is a joy that she will never know without Him.

There are millions of "Donnas" out there.
People who not only don't understand real joy but
aren't even sure they want it. People who find it easier
to cling to hurts than hope for healing. There are areas
in my life like that. How about yours?

How long has it been since you've closed your
eyes and pictured your Heavenly Father holding you
close, gently bouncing you while He kisses your
cheeks. I'll bet if you listen you will hear Him saying,
"I love you. I have wonderful plans for you . . ."
That's just how our Father is; He wants us to sense
and experience the joy He offers us.

God says this in Jeremiah 29:11–13 about you:
"For I know the plans I have for you. Plans to prosper
you and not to harm you, plans to give you hope and a
future. Then you will call upon me and come and pray
to me, and I will listen to you. You will seek me and
find me when you seek me with all your heart."

I hope Donna finds real joy.

$\mathcal{S}$piritual $\mathcal{S}$enses

Chapter Six Questions

$\mathcal{G}$etting to know you, getting to know all about you . . .

1. What is your favorite one-stop superstore?

2. What is your favorite holiday?

3. Can you think of a favorite "snow day" memory? Write about it, please.

It's time to apply!

*"One of the greatest tragedies among God's people is that, while they have a deep longing to experience God, they are experiencing God day after day **but do not know how to recognize Him.**"*
Henry T. Blackaby, Experiencing God

4. Do you see God working in your life right now? What's He up to?

5. Let's take this a step further (I know, you're saying, "Goodie!"). Write down the names of three people you feel closest to. Next to each name briefly write something you see God doing, right now, in their lives.

Person #1 -

Person #2 -

Person #3 -

6. Read John 5:17. What does this verse assure us of?

7. Read 1 Kings 19:11–13. What do you learn about the Lord's presence here?

Yes, God is always at work around us and in us, but His presence isn't always as obvious as a storm, fire, or earthquake. His work and presence can also be gentle and quiet. That's why we need to exchange our physical senses for spiritual ones.

The Lord reminded people many times in scripture not to limit their senses to the physical, but to begin hearing and seeing spiritually. We often find Jesus telling a story that seemed simple, often about agriculture so everyone could relate, and then He would end it with, "He who has ears to hear, let him hear." (Mark 4:1–9, for example.)

8. Read these next couple of illustrations and record how Jesus saw passed the physical surface and got to the spiritual heart-of-the-matter in these people's lives.

John 4:7–26 (This should be familiar!):

Matthew 19:16–26:

9. How would your day change if you used your spiritual senses?

Journaling Time

Remember my day at Wal-Mart? Journal about a time when you have shown the tenderness of God to someone, like the father holding his son.

Journal about a time you gave the gift of forgiveness, love, or mercy to someone who needed it. Were you excited to give it, like the couple in Wal-Mart, or did you give it grudgingly with strings attached?

Journal about a time you were able to show the joy of the Lord, even in the depths of hurt or sorrow.

" . . . Look around you! Vast fields are ripening all around us and are ready now for the harvest. The harvesters are paid good wages, and the fruit they harvest is people brought to eternal life. What joy awaits both the planter and the harvester alike! You know the saying, 'One person plants and someone else harvests.' And it's true. I sent you to harvest where you didn't plant; others had already done the work, and you will gather the harvest."
John 4:35 - 38

Let's Pray . . .

Lord, Thank You for working all around me! Just as You love and pursue a relationship with me, You are doing the same in the lives all around me! The vastness of Your love is astounding. I adore you!

Father, today I learned this:

Holy Spirit, remind me this week of these things:

Jesus, our relationship will benefit from these changes because:

Section Three

REMEMBERING YOUR ROLE

"Cheeseburgers, Steppingstones, and Tinkle"

My husband Paul is the strong-silent type. That's exactly opposite of me. I'm the mushy-loud type. I talk a lot and have even found, unfortunately, that I can still be understood with my whole foot stuck in my mouth. It's amazing! Some people have those tiny retainers in their mouth and can no longer speak clearly, but me . . . an entire size eight and a half foot, and I can still be heard and understood perfectly.

I guess that's why I love this story I'm about to share.

One Sunday morning, while I was still lying in bed wishing for something that made me look thirty pounds lighter to wear, Paul and Adam were getting ready in our bathroom. As Sunday mornings usually go, we were feeling rushed and tempers were starting to rise. I listened to my oldest and my husband banter back and forth. Paul was telling Adam to leave the bathroom and Adam was starting to get sassy. Paul can take a lot, but I knew his limit was coming - and I knew it wouldn't be pretty.

Sure enough, one more snotty comment from Adam brought a long, deep breath from Paul. That could only mean one thing. The strong-silent type was about to blow! I boarded up the windows and headed for the basement as Adam's life surely passed before his little eyes. I thought, as I gathered my other children, I'm really going to miss that kid.

When Paul's lungs reached maximum capacity, his thunderous voice bellowed out across the land,

"ADAM PAUL JANSEN!
YOU DON'T TALK TO ME THAT WAY!
I AM YOUR *MOTHER!*!"

I held my breath. "Did I just hear that right?" I asked myself.

Silence covered the house. Nobody knew what

to do. Finally, brave or very, very foolish, little Adam said with a quivering voice, "You're, you're . . . my *Mother?*"

Paul started to chuckle. Then we both started to roar! Adam fell on the floor laughing as the rest of the Jansens joined in. We snickered and hooted at this big, strong man's confusion of his role in the family. I knew Paul admired me, I just didn't realize he actually wanted to **BE** me!

It was so nice to be at the other end of a speaking faux pas, for once. But, you know, this scenario about the confusion of our roles in the family and in our relationships isn't always funny—especially in our relationship with God.

In our last sections, we've focused on the certainty of God's exciting plans for our lives and His amazing love for each of us. Those are important aspects of our relationship with God and I, personally, love to be reminded of those things. It makes me feel warm and fuzzy. However, when we only get to know the "warm fuzzy" side of our relationship with God, we can lose sight of His authority over us.

"The fear of the Lord is the beginning of wisdom . . ." says Psalm 111:10. There is a vital balance in understanding that God is unfathomable in His holiness and yet is willing to be our friend. He holds the authority of eternity in the same hand that He tenderly carries the widow and the weak.

God is holy, magnificent, tremendous, and righteous. He loves to lavish His love upon us and lead us with assurance. Not because we are so great, but because He is so great. It's important to remember our *role* in our relationship with God. He is our friend, but certainly not our equal.

Surely, as Adam stood face-to-face with his dad in the bathroom that Sunday morning, watching his dad draw a long breath; he indeed feared his father. Not because Paul is a harsh, unfriendly dad - no, on the contrary, Paul is kind and loving to all of us. Adam feared his dad because he understood he had done wrong, and he also understood his dad had the power to punish him. **Adam had a healthy fear of his father's authority**. Adam understands his role in the family.

Now if only Paul could remember which role is his.

Chapter Seven

MIXED-UP THINKING!

*"When I consider your heavens, the work of
your fingers, the moon and the stars,
which you have set in place,
what is man that you are
mindful of him . . . ?"*
Psalm 8:3–4

One night Joey and I went to fetch dinner for
our families at a local fast-food restaurant on their
"forty-nine cent cheeseburger" night. We needed a
total of sixteen cheeseburgers between our two clans.
I pulled up to the intercom and heard the voice of

a young man say, "Welcome, can I take your order, please?"

"Sure", I answered. "I'll take sixteen cheeseburgers and . . ."

"Oh, ma'am," the lad interrupted, "we can't take an order for any more than ten cheeseburgers per car."

"Well," I reasoned, "we're ordering for two families in here. I'll just put this on two separate orders."

Pause. "Just a minute . . ." said the teen-ager. Joey and I could hear him discuss our dilemma with his manager because, in all the excitement, he forgot to stop pressing the walkie-talkie button that connects the common world to burger world. After receiving council he said to us, "No, you can only order ten cheeseburgers per car."

Rolling my eyes at Joey I decided to go to battle. I strapped on my combat boots and said to the boy, "Okay, I'll tell you what I'm gonna do. I'll take ten cheeseburgers now, and then I'll pull my van around again and order six more."

Pause. "Just a minute," said a boy destined to quit his job. Once again, Joey and I were privileged to hear another brief burger-rule conversation with the manager. The lad came back with a commanding voice, "No, we can't do that. Only ten cheeseburgers per car."

Seeing the look on my face, Joey curled herself up into the fetal position in the passenger seat. She knew the battle wouldn't be ending just yet. Cheeseburgers didn't even sound tasty anymore but this injustice must be challenged! I **HAD** to give this boy trouble; it was my duty as an American! Today it may only be cheeseburgers, but tomorrow they may try to limit my chocolate consumption. Over my dead body!

Remaining calm, I added a dash of authority to my voice, "O.K. kid. I'll order ten cheeseburgers now, and then I'll drive home and get my other car. Then I'll drive back here and order six more cheeseburgers."

Pause. "Just a minute."

After yet another short dialogue with his manager, the brainwashed boy responded, "No, there has to be a *two hour time lapse* between orders for the same person."

While Joey tried to climb into the glove compartment, my mind instantly raced with the tedious task of charting such detailed information during "forty-nine cent cheeseburger night." Could there possibly be an enormous McWall plastered with Polaroid pictures documenting each person who ordered, how many cheeseburgers they bought, the time they ordered, and the type of car they were driving? How absurd!

I took a deep, soothing chest-full of air and said, "Sir, do you realize how dumb this is?"

Pause. "Uh . . . just a minute," he said.

To hurry this war along, and to be wise with the taxpayers' money, I ordered ten cheeseburgers and pulled ahead to the second window with fake submission. I reminded myself not to take the bag until I saw the whites of his McEyes. Pulling to a stop, I took my cheeseburgers from the shaky hands of a poor, confused young soldier. "Now, this is just craziness," I said with a dangerous grin. "I want you to know that I'll be pulling back around to order six more cheeseburgers. I hope you won't mind."

I rounded the circle again and ordered the six remaining burgers pretending not to recognize the voice of my rival. Approaching the second window, for the second time, I wondered if I would be greeted by the same young man or by a police officer ready to handcuff me for illegal cheeseburger accumulation. Thankfully it was just the same old kid. Aiming for peace I said, "Hey, don't I know you from somewhere?" Whimsical humor wasn't the right choice. The boy leaned toward me, trying to cram as much of his McHead through the little McWindow as possible. He put his hand over his lop-sided microphone, blocking out burger world, and whispered right at me with angry breath, "I better not lose my job over this!" I smirked, still hoping he was kidding . . . he was dead-faced. I handed him my money wadded into the shape of a hand grenade and took my black-market bag of burgers from his clutched fist. I drove off toward home with my crumpled-up sister-in-law. The war had been hard on her.

Joey was able to return to her human form as soon we pulled out of the parking lot and we both fought to breath between fits of laughter. What an absurdity! What a crazy, mixed-up rule! What a pity that that boy probably spit on my cheeseburgers! I decided not to eat any. I don't care much for McSpit.

Fast-food places aren't the only ones with mixed-up thinking. Have you ever visited the Internet site called: www.dumblaws.com.? The name says it all. Here are some examples of laws that are, or were at one time, on the books:

TEXAS:

* A city ordinance states that a person cannot go barefoot without first obtaining a special five-dollar permit.

* A recently passed anticrime law requires criminals to give their victims twenty-four hours

notice, either orally or in writing, and to explain the nature of the crime to be committed. (Though not legally enforced, it's also a nice touch to send a "thank you" note afterwards.)

* In Port Arthur, Texas, obnoxious odors may not be emitted while in an elevator. (Many of my own family members would be serving life sentences if they lived in Port Arthur!)

NEW YORK:

* It is against the law to throw a ball at someone's head for fun.

* The penalty for jumping off a building is . . . death.

* Slippers are not to be worn after 10:00 P.M. (Can you imagine being in prison and someone asking you, "Hey, what're ya in for?")

KENTUCKY:

* It's illegal to transport an ice-cream cone in your pocket.

* A woman may not buy a hat without her

husband's permission. (I believe it was my husband who wrote this law.)

ILLINOIS:
* Law forbids eating in a place that's on fire.

* Ice skating at the Riverside pond during the months of June and August is prohibited. (No comment.)

* It is against the law to make faces at dogs. (Now cats are another story.)

INDIANA (my home state):
* Baths may not be taken between the months of October and March. (My children have this law framed in their bathroom.)

* Within four hours of eating garlic, a person may not enter a movie house, theater, or ride a public streetcar.

* It's illegal to make a monkey smoke a cigarette. (Now what will my family and I do on Friday nights?)

****

How's that for mixed-up thinking? Mixed up thinking is everywhere! In our states, towns, restaurants, homes, and yes . . . even our own hearts.

In this book we're looking at the relationship God offers us through Jesus Christ. Romans 5:6–12 holds the tremendous news that though we're sinners, the Holy God offers us an intimate friendship with Him through His Son. Friendship with God through Jesus! Just between you and me, I think they could have done better. The whole invitation seems a little mixed-up. God doesn't even want us to keep our affiliation with Him a secret. He's not ashamed of us! He desires our friendship to be experienced so thoroughly that it spills out of our lives and into the lives of others. Through following Him boldly and joining Him in ministry our lives become a display of God's glory.

God wanted to use the people of Israel as a display of His glory. After years of captivity and slavery in Egypt, God called Moses to lead the Israelites to a land of their own. Exodus records this amazing journey with its wide-variety of plagues, the parting of the Red Sea, God's gracious leading from a cloud, a tremendous amount of whining and complaining from the Israelites, and all the birds you could eat. And that's only the first two months of travel!

In chapter 19:3–8, we find Moses, the exhausted but faithful friend of God, climbing up a mountain to talk with his Lord. God called to him and said, "Give these instructions to the descendants of Jacob, the people of Israel: 'You have seen what I did to the Egyptians. You know how I brought you to myself and carried you on eagle's wings. Now if you will obey me and keep my covenant, you will be my own special treasure from among all the nations of the earth; for all the earth belongs to me. And you will be to me a kingdom of priests, my holy nation."

With such a wonderful promise, no wonder the Israelites honored God for the rest of their lives, never departing from His will. No wonder they followed God with earnest hearts until their dying day. Oh wait . . . I believe I'm a little mixed-up.

The truth is, disobedience and rebellion were the prominent features of the Israelites' story. The Bible reveals a repetitious cycle of God's forgiveness, the Israelites' hard-heartedness and sin, God's anger, the Israelites' repentance, again followed by God's mercy and forgiveness. As predictable as a merry-go-round, the forgiveness always seemed to be followed by more rebellion. Finally, after a series of rebellion, repentance, and forgiveness reruns, God has another heart-to-heart discussion with Moses in Exodus 32:7–10. Keep in mind as you read this, this is the same God, talking to the same Moses, about the same Israelites.

> *"Then the Lord said to Moses, 'Go down, because your* (notice the "your") *people, whom you* (notice the "you") *brought up out of Egypt, have become corrupt. They have been quick to turn away from what I commanded them and have made themselves an idol cast in the shape of a calf. They have bowed down to it and sacrificed to it and have said, 'These are your gods, O Israel, who brought you up out of Egypt.'*

> *"'I have seen these people,' the Lord said to Moses, 'and they are a stiff-necked people. Now leave me alone so that my anger may burn against them and that I may destroy them. **Then I will make** you **into a great nation.'** "*

Have you, as a parent, ever seen your child making foolish choices and with a broken heart you say to your husband, "Look at what *your* children have done! No, those aren't *my* kids! Those are *your* kids!"? In Exodus 32:7–10, we see this kind of parental despair lurching in God's holy anger. While human parents undoubtedly fail their children often, God had never once failed to provide for, protect, or forgive His Israelite children. Knowing this, how much more must God have ached over these pitiful, ungrateful kids? I imagine as He watched His Israelites prostitute their worship to a lifeless image of a cow, He must have turned His face and said, "No, these are *your* people, Moses."

Oh, but God is so faithful! He had promised to make a great, holy nation out of Israel - *if* they were obedient. Even though Israel failed miserably to honor God, God would still make good on His promise. For Him, fruition didn't require a mass of people. He was ready to fulfill His promise through one faithful man, Moses.

God didn't need the Israelites in order to accomplish His plan. However, out of His great grace, God invited the Israelites to join Him. **The Israelites hard-heartedness thwarted *their* future possibilities, not God's.** God didn't need the Israelites; He wanted them.

God doesn't need you. That's the reality. God wants you. That's the mystery.

God has a plan that He's inviting you to be a part of, too. If you will be faithful to Him, He will bring about a marvelous display of His glory. Don't be like the Israelites and let your eyes wander off the spiritual journey and fix on the physical journey you're traveling. When we do this, we *stop* humbly thanking God for the chance to minister along side of Him, and *start* mumbling about how tired we are and how our traveling conditions aren't fair.

"Those third graders are just rotten during Sunday School. This church better be thankful I show up to teach!"

"I was up late every night this week getting these choir songs ready for Sunday and then only half the choir shows up. If nobody is going to appreciate my hard work, I'll just go somewhere else!"

"If I didn't know God needed me to work at this nursing home for Him, I'd split. The pay is awful, the people are too needy, and the food stinks. But hey, I'm doing it for God."

Busy lifestyles, lack of discernment, and good ole' guilt can change us from ministers to martyrs in the work God invites us to. It's a mixed-up heart that serves believing God now owes us something for stepping in and saving the day. Wouldn't you agree that a God who's able to part the Red Sea and throw fire down from Heaven could probably come up with plenty of Sunday School teachers, bus drivers, choir leaders, pastors, book writers, and child-care providers? The whole world is His, and yet, He called you. When you hear His invitation to serve along side

Him, be thankful. Remind yourself regularly of the privilege to have a Friend with such a tremendous promise and plan.

God doesn't need us, but praise His beautiful name, He wants us all! In fact, He wants us so badly that He gave His only Son so that we might have a relationship, an intimate friendship, with Him. (John 3:16) No matter how many times we may have traveled a merry-go-round of promise, failure, and redemption, we are invited to experience the exhilaration of a life lived for a God who can do immeasurable things through one faithful, willing soul.

I can't imagine living without that relationship—and there's nothing mixed-up about that!

Mixed-Up Thinking

Chapter Seven Questions

Getting to know you,
getting to know all about you . . .

1. Can you think of a rule that drove you crazy growing up? How about now?

2. If you could make one law, what would it be?

3. If you have children, when was a time you said, "Those can't be *my* children!"

It's time to apply!

Read Isaiah 40:12–31 and jot down several tremendous qualities of God.

Now read Revelation 1:12–16 and Revelation 4:1–11. This is a deep book and the apostle John had a hard time finding words that could accurately describe what he witnessed. Write down some of the amazing descriptions given of our awe-inspiring God.

4. The Israelites experienced the awesomeness of God first hand. They saw God send plagues on their enemies, miraculously lead them through the desert from a cloud, and provide for their needs. How could the Israelites, do you think, know of God's tremendous authority and yet *worry about their future, complain along their journey, and put other things before God?*

5. Do you identify more with Moses (faithful), or the Israelites (unfaithful)? How does this affect your relationship with God?

6. Circle the description that best describes the role of God in your life:

The awesome, righteous Authority of my life.

A friend that I enjoy talking to when I have time.

A stranger that I'm trying to get to know.

A force that I feel alienated from.

7. Are you content with that response? Why or Why not?

Journaling Time

Sometimes I ask my kids to help me with a chore. I don't do this because I need their help, in fact, I could probably get the job done faster and smoother by myself. I invite them to join me in work that needs done simply because I enjoy being with them. The time and the experience spent together adds character and depth to our relationship. Even if the task turns out to be a pain in the neck, which it most often does because of their fighting and complaining, I know that we have at least spent some time together. I may be threatening and grounding them, but hey - at least we're together!

Do you believe God enjoys spending time with you? Why or why not?

When have you felt like God opened your spiritual eyes to a need that you could help with? Did you want to do it? Did you do it?

If you followed through on what you felt the Lord calling you to, what did you learn from the experience? Did the Lord use it to help others grow spiritually?

You have read today of God's awesomeness. You more than likely can also name times where you experienced this awesomeness first hand in your life. Knowing of His tremendous authority, do you still **worry about your future, complain along the journey, and put other things before God?**

Come let us bow down in worship, let us kneel before the Lord our God our maker; for he is our God and we are the people of his pasture, the flock under his care. Psalms 95:6–7

Let's Pray . . .

Lord, You are my God! You are righteous, holy, splendid, good, loving, compassionate, gracious, merciful, divine, and best of all, You are mine, and I am Yours. I love You.

Father, today I learned this:

Holy Spirit, remind me this week of these things:

Jesus, our relationship will benefit from these changes because:

Chapter Eight

NOT ENOUGH!

*"So neither he who plants nor he who
waters is anything, but only God,
who makes things grow."*
1 Corinthians 3:7

One summer I decided to be a model mother
and do a spectacular craft with my kids, a project
that I'd be able to casually mention to my friends so
they would tell me what a creative, awesome mom I
was (I'm so godly). My children and I were going to
make garden steppingstones - complete with rocks,

imprints, and other goodies. Yes, it was going to be a day for the baby books.

First we went to buy some supplies. We needed rocks. Not ordinary dirt rocks—NO! We needed virgin rocks—the kind that have never been defiled by mud, slime, or extreme weather. Only the best would do for this project. In fact, I even decided that I would read the directions on my newly purchased bag of cement. Reading directions is something I usually view as a huge waste of time and avoid all together. However, today was special. Today Melissa Ann Jansen will read directions and acquire virgin stones!

There were other things to take care of, not just rocks and cement. I had to burrow through the rubbish in my closet to find several shirt boxes that I could line with Saran Wrap. The kids had the chore of searching the yard for special leaves, sticks, and small animals that could be smashed into their masterpieces. And lastly, I had to mix and pour the cement into our boxes - not too shallow, not too deep. Everything was progressing beautifully, just like the directions said they would.

Finally, we were ready to decorate our stepping stones!— Oh, the children and I laughed together while we worked and admired each other's work. We were a darling family, not a bad one in the bunch. Everyone was truly enjoying our steppingstone project and it was all too soon when we found ourselves finished. I suggested that we lay them all out on the driveway, where they would be safe, to dry. While we waited, I went in the house to do some chores—whistling.

It was a wonderful day! The sun was shining. The children were laughing. The steppingstones were drying. The mother was dancing. The child was screaming. Hey, the child is screaming? What's that all about!? Screaming wasn't supposed to be a part of our day. I read the directions and they said nothing about screaming children!

I ran outside. One of my boys stood frozen and tear-stained. He was trying to tell me what happened but all his words blubbered together. I looked to my other two children for guidance, "What's he saying? What's he saying?"

After consulting my crying child translation book I decoded my son's words: "Uncle Chris just ran over our steppingstones! I glared at our hallowed stones then over at my brother, who was doubled over laughing and saying between breaths, "I'm sorry! I'm so sorry!" It all started to sink in. My brother had pulled in for a visit and accidentally parted our stepping-stones like the Red Sea.

I wanted to be mad, really I did. But it was all so pathetic: the crying child, the parted stones, the virgin rocks now corrupted and cemented to the tread of my brother's tires. I couldn't help it; I busted out laughing.

All that work . . . ruined. For once in my life I had followed every direction and it was all for nothing.

You know, sometimes parenting can be a lot like this steppingstone project. As parents, we can try to do everything right. We can read all the right books. We can discipline exactly like Dr. Dobson recommends. We can say all the right things. We can send our kids to the perfect schools. We can be godly examples. We can follow every direction and piece of wisdom available to us and still, life can roll right over our children, leaving them imprinted and broken.

My dad shared a story with me about a very prominent Christian man who had several children. Throughout these children's teenage years, each child had lived for the Lord; all except one. This godly man and his wife had seemingly tried everything to reach their wayward child and were left exhausted. Finally, at the point of yet another crisis with this child in the middle of the night, the father had nothing left to offer. No words left to say. No punishment left to give. Instead he stared at his son, told him he forgave and loved him, and walked away. Climbing back into bed, the couple lay depleted before God and gave this child completely over to Him.

As I listened to my dad relay this story, the hairs on my neck (am I supposed to have hair on my neck?) stood on end. Up until that precise moment I had never really thought about the possibility that my children might someday be rebellious. I guess I had been living under a fairy tale spell that had duped me into believing that as long as Paul and I loved the Lord, and lived a life that reflected that love, surely our children would love Him, too. That illusion quickly crumbled as I listened, all hairy-necked, to a story about a man who despite his close walk with God had experienced the heartache of an unsaved, rebellious child.

As a young mother, this grave discovery was a heart-full to think about. For Paul and me - our most burning desire is that our children would live for the Lord. My mind began to flood with events Paul and I needed to plan, rules we needed to set up, and immediate actions that needed to be taken to save our children from impending rebellion!

I can't honestly remember how much time I spent with a heavy heart over this rude awakening. Night after night, I walked around our neighborhood talking out loud with the Lord, trying to pinpoint **what Paul and I needed to do** or **whom we needed to be** to assure our children's spiritual futures. Why did some children from ungodly homes grow up loving the Lord, while others from godly homes denied the faith? The whole subject was a bitter pill and I spent a lot of time trying to choke it down before I felt like the Lord gave me some helpful insight.

Do you want to hear the truth I finally embraced? Do you want to know what I believe that we as parents, grandparents, aunts, and uncles, can *do* or *be* to **guarantee** our children will have a love relationship with the Lord? Are you ready?

Nothing.

Nothing—isn't that groundbreaking? I finally came to the conclusion that *there is nothing that Paul and I can do or become that will be enough to guarantee our children's salvation*. Nothing. Do you know why? Because we, Paul and I, simply are not enough. In fact, you're not enough either. In regards to your child/grandchild coming to know the Lord, you are simply not enough.

You're not enough. Isn't that an encouraging motto! Stand up right now and shout it out loud, "**I am not enough**!" Don't you feel empowered? Maybe I should put out one of those motivational tapes so on the way to work you could listen to me say over and over, "You are not enough. You are not enough." I think it'd be a big seller.

If you don't have any children you might be thinking, "What does this have to do with me?"

Friend, if you're a Christian, it's your responsibility to spiritually nurture those people God places in your path: a child, niece or nephew, friend, coworker, or "enemy." Although I'm focusing on parents and children, being physically childless doesn't exempt you from nurturing others as long as you're a Christian.

Our role in nurturing and discipleship is huge. Trying to adequately cover it in this book would be like trying to cover all of me with my high school bikini - it simply can **not** be done. Still, let's try covering it in modest fashion, with three basic points.

Point number one is: You are not enough.

This motto is review, I realize, but it must be said again. How do I know you're not enough? Because the Bible says in Romans 3:23 that "all fall short of the glory of God." We all fail. There probably isn't a day that goes by that you couldn't easily find failure's fingerprints on me. Knowing this about myself increases my concern for the souls of my children; knowing my husband, Paul, makes me worry even more. (Smile!)

God entrusted Paul and Melissa Jansen with three beautiful souls born in Adam Paul, Ryan

Solomon, and Madison Joanna. He's entrusted you with someone too—maybe several someones. Whether it's our children we are trying to lead to the kingdom of Heaven or some other person, the first truth we must recognize is that we are not enough—not today, not tomorrow. I don't care how godly you are, or think you are, eventually you're going to fail. If your hope for someone's salvation is rooted in you and your example, be ready to be disappointed because you are not enough.

Let me also say that if the security of your own faith is rooted in someone other than Jesus Christ, be ready to be disappointed, because eventually every human will fail.

Point number two: What you do is not enough.

Parents, grandparents, aunts, and uncles get caught in the same mousetrap time and time again. We fool ourselves into thinking that if we can only **DO** all the right things; our children will surely live for the Lord. We say:

"Let's put them in home school."

"Let's enroll them in Christian classes."

"Let's take them on mission trips."

"Let's make sure they never miss a week of church."

"Let's always schedule a time set-aside to just talk with our children."

"Let's show them tough-love."

"Let's show them grace."

"Let's make sure to read scripture to them every day."

"Let's take them to work in the homeless shelter this Christmas."

"Let's, let's, let's!"

All of these things can be wonderful! Each and every one can be a beneficial, worthwhile thing to do. My point is this: *If your hope for someone's salvation is rooted in "doing the right things", be ready to be disappointed, because it's not enough.*

So what should we do? Should we say, "What's the use? Why not live however I want? I'll never be enough—or do enough—so why try?"

The apostle Paul provides much insight into grace and the part it plays in our relationship with God. In Ephesians 2:8–9 he writes, "For it is by grace you have been saved, through faith - and this not from yourselves, it is the gift of God - not by works, so that no one can boast." If my relationship with God depended on me—**who I am** and **what I do**—I would have no hope. No matter how good I grow to be or how many good things I am involved in, it will never be enough. I can only enter into a relationship with God by the grace extended through Jesus Christ.

So is this grace a license to sin? No! (Romans 6:1–2) When we live for the Lord we ought to strive, out of obedience, love, and respect, to please God by being like Jesus. **The secret is remembering our weaknesses while clinging to His strength.** Securing our hope in Him, not in who we are or what we do. Because: (1) we are not enough, and (2) the things we do are not enough.

In this same way, God has blessed us with relationships with our children. As parents we ought to strive - out of obedience, love, and respect - to please God by being like Jesus to our children. The quality of person we are, the decisions we make, the way we discipline, the words we say - all these things should be edifying to our children. But while we are living this way our hope can not become foolishly rooted in ourselves, it absolutely must be humbly and gratefully rooted in our God.

Ahhh, point number three is coming. Have you already seen it peeking its beautiful head around the corner? Here it comes:

Point number three: God IS enough!

Thank the wonderful Lord, there **is** hope. This hope is in our Lord. Only God is enough. We **WILL** fail. The things we do **WILL** fail. But God **WILL NEVER** fail! **He is where our hope belongs.**

Growing up, I can remember many people asking my mom and dad for parenting advice. These, most definitely, were people who had never met my brothers and me! The simple, reliable, and seemingly-boring response my parents faithfully replied was this: "Pray." Sometimes, because the people expected a little more lively and lengthy answer, my parents would add the importance of laughing together and effective communication, etc. But their first response was always, "Pray."

I'm honored to tell you that my parents followed their own advice faithfully. I remember many quiet nights as a child, lying in my bed and listening to the sweet lullaby of my parents' prayers for my brothers and me. As an adult, I'm so thankful for the little house I did most of my growing up in, with its little bedrooms almost piled on top of each other. Without it, I would not have had the privilege of falling asleep to the sound of soft, reverent voices belonging to two people who were devoted enough to pray for me.

You see, my parents understood that their best chance of seeing their children grow into a personal relationship with the Lord was to humble themselves daily before God. They played an effective discipleship role by realizing that Ken and Judy Mishler were **helpers** in the spiritual journeys of Chris, Doug, and Melissa—not the **hope**.

Remember the story I began with about the father who had tried everything to bring his child back from rebellion? Well, the night the father gave his son completely over to God and extended God's grace to his hurting child, the son was finally broken. He was overwhelmed by the grace of his earthly father *and* his Heavenly Father. Perhaps it won't even surprise you to hear that this young man is now in fulltime Christian ministry.

Isn't the Lord wonderful! *Our children are never in a more secure place than when we lay them at His feet in prayer.* Paul and I want to live godly lives for our children to see. We want to listen and laugh with our kids and impress upon them the importance of rooting themselves in Scripture. But more than anything else, we want to cover them in prayer. You see, God is where our hope resides. And praise be to God, **He is enough!**

Now, what am I going to do with these mangled stepping-stones?

$\mathcal{N}$ ot $\mathcal{E}$ nough

Chapter Eight Questions

$\mathcal{G}$ etting to know you,
getting to know all about you.

1. What's the best "craft" you've ever made? Where is it today?

2. Have you ever followed all the directions and still end up with a flop? Describe that experience. Did you ever try the project again?

Melissa Jansen

It's time to apply!
"I have no greater joy than to hear that my children are walking in the truth."
3 John 1:4

3. Write three names of people (children, neighbors, etc.) that you feel God has placed in your life for you to spiritually nurture or disciple. How are you being faithful to that call?

I always admire the apostle Paul for the genuine fatherly love he had for the churches that God had him invest himself in. When he and his traveling companions ministered to a church they gave whole-heartedly of themselves. They fervently taught people about Jesus, most who had never been offered a relationship with God before, let alone one based on grace and not on works! When Paul would leave a church he eagerly awaited a report to hear that the church was doing well. When he knew word was coming to him, he seemed like an expectant father, pacing up and down the hall nervously, waiting for the news.

Paul longed to hear the church was still growing

in the Lord. He wanted to know that they hadn't fallen for false teachings or became slaves to rules and meaningless customs. As their father, he dreamed of their freedom in Christ and did all he could to protect his spiritual children. When he was with them he taught them and modeled a Christ-centered life, but ultimately, he had to release them and simply trust the Lord.

Look up these verses about what Paul passionately did for his "children". Summarize the main thoughts in these verses:

Philippians 1:3–6

Colossians 1:3–4

Colossians 1:9–12

1 Thessalonians 1:2–3

2 Thessalonians 1:11–12

Philemon 1:4–6

4. Do you see any areas that Paul covered in prayer for his spiritual children that you need to incorporate in your prayers?

1) We are not enough!
2) The things we do are not enough!
3) God is enough!

5. When we are talking about our children coming to know God intimately, why is it so important to remember that only God is enough?

Journaling Time

Knowing that Paul and I are not enough, and the things we do are not enough - we pray regularly for God to fill-in the "pot holes," the areas that we fail in, of our parenting. Some days we substitute the word "pot-holes" for craters, chasms, or great, cavernous abysses - depending how rotten we have parented for the day. For me, praying that prayer replaces my focus on the Lord. It mysteriously exchanges my anxiety (because of my failings) for a great peace (because of God's sovereignty).

Another thing that I have found helpful while praying for my children is to work down a "suggested areas of prayer" list given to me years ago. We covered several areas already, suggested by the apostle Paul, but perhaps you will find this list useful as well. Certainly, this list is not to be treated as "sure-thing" directions but useful for re-focusing on God's intervention in many specific areas.

10 ways to pray for our children:

1. Thanksgiving for the opportunity to minister to each child in your life.

2. That they will know Christ as Lord and Savior early in life.

3. That they will have a hatred for sin.

4. That they will be protected from the evil one in each area of their lives: spiritual, emotional, physical, mental, and sexual.

5. That they will have a responsible attitude.

6. That they will respect those in authority over them.

7. That they will desire the right kind of friends and be protected from the wrong friends.

8. That they will be kept from the wrong mate and saved for the right one.

9. That they will be caught when guilty and willing to repent.

10. That they will be single hearted, willing to be completely sold-out for Jesus.

Let's Pray . . .

Lord, Thank you for allowing me to be used as a "Help" in the discipleship of those around me, but never let me forget that You are the only "Hope". Thank You for your faithfulness and perfect example. Thank You for drawing me to You and forgiving me for all the ways I fail You. You're awesome!

Father, today I learned this:

Holy Spirit, remind me this week of these things:

Jesus, our relationship will benefit from these changes because:

Chapter Nine

WISDOM WORTH AGING FOR!

*"Oh, the depth of the riches of the wisdom
and knowledge of God!
How unsearchable his judgments,
and his paths beyond tracing out!"*
Romans 11:33

A couple of years ago, I entered my thirties and I've decided I don't like it. This aging thing isn't fun anymore! Many years ago I would actually count down the slow, sluggish days until I could officially add another year to my age total. Now I dress in black and mourn. That's okay though, black makes me look thinner.

At my surprise thirtieth birthday party, I was privileged to endure jokes from friends (who, by the way, are ALL OLDER than I am) about being old and going downhill. They bought me presents like denture cream, support hose with a built-in bra, and enemas. Have you ever tried to return an enema? The sales clerk asked me if there was anything wrong with it. I told her it was a gift but I already had one in that color.

There are some people who say growing older doesn't bother them. My mother used to be one of those people (AKA, "liars"). My mom faithfully claimed she was excited about aging until a recent doctor's appointment that revealed she'd shrunk two feet since her last visit. How could we have overlooked this? If she continues to shrink at such a rate she'll be about six inches tall by Christmas. I'm actually quite excited about the thought of it. I've already started to sing, "All I want for Christmas is my six-inch mom . . ."

It's not just shrinking that I dread about growing older. There are many things that go obnoxiously awry with the body as we age. Although I'm only at the beginning of this process I've already noticed some shifting and dragging going on. For instance:

*When I was a teenager I would lay down exhausted after I swam laps in the pool. Now just bathing wears me out.

*When I was younger and I wanted to weigh myself, I'd slip off my shoes and step on the scale. Now I not only lose the shoes - but the pants, shirt, and socks as well. Then I trim my bangs and exfoliate my entire body, hoping to lose a couple pounds of dead skin. I make quite a scene at the doctor's office.

*Another big change is, after having three children; even light running is a challenge. When the phone rings and I run to get it, **I *tinkle* in my pants with each step!** Yeah, I said it . . . I tinkle! Isn't that humiliating? I have to keep a fresh change of clothes by each phone.

Oh, there are other loathsome changes. Sneaking into church late is impossible now because my pantyhose make that terrible "swish - swish" sound when I walk. My only chance is to sneak-in during prayer, hobbling toward my pew with my knees spaced farther apart like I'm getting ready to mount a horse. I wouldn't recommend this though, because some Christian-rebels pray with their eyes open and they'll catch you! The easy answer is to stop wearing pantyhose altogether but I read that they make you look five pounds lighter. I now wear seven pairs at a time . . . that's thirty-five pounds folks.

Putting on all those hose may be why I'm late for church.

But you know what? Aging also has its perks. There's a kind of pride that comes with growing more comfortable in your own skin. With its distinct scars and bulges, my body is beginning to tell the story of my life - like an old army veteran with battle scars. The longer we live, our temporary bodies will undoubtedly start to bear the "war stories" we've been through.

I've always liked scars. I like the stories they tell. I like something I can touch and see to remind me of experiences I've been through. However, cut knees and scraped elbows are one thing . . . scars on our hearts are quite another.

As surely as our bodies tell the story of living, our hearts can also bear the marks of years and events. Sometimes hands have touched us in uninvited ways, branding us with fingerprints of shame. Maybe ugly words have dug their razor-sharp claws deep into our souls, wounding our sense of self. Perhaps we've been hurt by unexpected situations that have left us crying quietly in the middle of the night, searching for answers.

I've spent nights quietly crying. I'll bet you have too. You should have called me, we could have cried together. When you were crying, were you like me, wondering what you were supposed to learn from the experience; wondering why God hadn't chose to step in and change the outcome?

In this section, we're examining God's role of authority in our lives. First we looked at His authoritative role in the ministry opportunities we are presented with. Next we looked at His authoritative role in the spiritual nurturing of people placed in our lives. In this chapter we're examining His authoritative role in the trials of our lives.

I remember a night I was lying awake in bed, long after Paul had fallen asleep. My heart was so sad that I actually felt raw inside. Wet, warm tears welled up in my eyes and I started to cry. These weren't the kind of tears you wipe off your cheeks, they were the kind you let run slowly down your face and rest on the pillow beside you.

My sorrow was deep because I had just been involved in an accident in which my van struck and killed a motorcyclist. Feelings of despair, confusion, and anguish (just to name a few), clung to me tighter than my skin. Every time I closed my eyes I saw the accident happening over and over again. In the quietness, I heard the awful sounds unmercifully echoing in my head. I ached, and felt guilty for that aching, knowing there was a grieving family hurting more than I could even imagine.

Melissa Jansen

That night I wanted terribly to be able to make some sense of all this trouble and pain. Finally, I got up and went to my office to try to write down my feelings. I sat down in my quiet house with noisy thoughts racing in my head. As I fought for words, a warm sense of peace came over me while I gave my questions, and my lack of understanding, over to God. This is what I wrote:

* * * * *

How *comforting* it is to know that my hands don't have to be big enough to protect. **H**ow *reassuring* it is to know that my mind doesn't have to comprehend tomorrow. **H**ow *consoling* it is to know that my eyes don't have to see what is ahead of me or **make sense** of what I have already seen. **H**ow *calming* it is to know that my life is not in my own control.

Not because I believe in small-minded thinking.
Not because I believe in a dormant existence.
Not because I don't consider myself
a capable processor.

It's because there is so much peace in knowing that my little hands rest in the big hands of a loving Protector. *It's because* my imprisoned mind can roam free within the vastness of my Father's thinking. *It's because* my blinded eyes can be amazed by the astounding vision of my Creator.

That Creator who dreams about me. That Father who loved me before anyone else ever knew me. That Daddy who holds me in the quiet of the night while I cry.

He is my life.
He is my daydream. He is my protector.
He is my Savior.
He is my future. He is my Lord.
He is my love.
He is my abundance. He is my everything.
<u>How blessed I am to know Him.</u>

It's so soothing not to have to know why I have life, **but Who Life is.**

* * * * *

There were many questions that I wanted answers for that night. **Even though God didn't give me peace by telling me the answers; He helped me make peace with my questions.**

*"For my thoughts are not your thoughts,
neither are your ways my ways,"
declares the Lord. "As the heavens are
higher than the earth, so are my ways higher*

than your ways and my thoughts
higher than your thoughts."
Isaiah 55:8

You see ladies, that night at my computer when my insides were dying; I started to feel reconciled to God's role of authority in the tragedies of my life. Many well-meaning people offered me a truck-load of reasons why God chose not to change the outcome. I found peace, however, in the basic fact that God is God. **His role in our tragedies is that of a higher power of thinking, a deeper source of healing, and a greater purpose for living.**

The mere fact that it was okay for me not to understand the "whys," *because God already did,* gave me peace.

George Washington Carver lived a remarkable life, full of adventure and purpose. His brilliance was attracted especially to the peanut, and George came up with over three hundred uses for it. I love the little story he tells when an admirer asked him how he thought of all those ideas he had for peanuts. Here's how George answered:

"One morning while I walked through the woods (George would get up and walk through the woods at four in the morning) I was talking to God. I said "Mr. Creator, what was the universe made for?"

"You want to know too much," God answered. "Your mind is too small to know that much."

Then I asked Him, "Mr. Creator, what was man made for?"

"Little man," God said, "you still want to know too much."

Then I asked Him to tell me about the peanut. "Mr. Creator, what is the peanut for?"

"That's more like it!" God said.

God's thinking is not our own. Sometimes we have questions bigger than our minds can understand. When we find ourselves struggling for answers we may simply need to trust God and be thankful for the peanuts we can comprehend.

Ironically, looking at my own life, the things that have brought the most despair and pain have ended up adding the most character and wisdom.

*"We also rejoice in our sufferings, because
we know that suffering produces
perseverance, perseverance, character;
and character, hope."*
Romans 5:3–4

Several years have passed now since that terrible accident in my life and I still have many "whys;" I'm sure that's true for all involved. I do know, however, that God has worked through that experience, just as I'm sure He's worked through the scarring experiences in your life. It's amazing that as the Authority over all of life, God can take the foulest memories, the deepest wounds, and the most unspeakable hurts in your life and bring peace. You may never look back on those scars and feel happy or even understand all you've endured, **but you can have peace.** It's the peace that comes when you rest in the hands of Someone bigger than you.

Yes, our bodies are gradually changing and transforming with age. Hopefully our hearts are doing some changing and transforming, too. Our goals, desires, purposes, and passions should all be a reflection of the wisdom we have gleaned over the years through our encounters in life, and even more, through our encounters with the One Who *is* Life.

My prayer for you is that with every wrinkle, scar, and gray hair that adds itself to your lovely body over the years, wisdom and peace will spring up with it.

Wisdom Worth Aging For

Chapter Nine Questions

Getting to know you,
getting to know all about you . . .

1. Have you enjoyed your aging process so far? What is one change, added to your body because of aging, that you are happy for? What is one change, added to your body because of aging, that you are not so tickled about?

2. How about the inner aging . . . maturing? What is one thing that has changed inside you over the years

that you are thankful for? Is there anything changing for the negative? If so, what is it?

3. What would be your best advice to a younger woman about aging? If you yourself are very young, what is a question about aging that you are wanting to know?

It's time to apply!

"When I was a child, I talked like a child, I thought like a child, I reasoned like a child. When I became a man, I put childish ways behind me."
1 Corinthians 13:11 NIV

Most people mature naturally in their character as they age. Often times though, when we face a trauma in our lives it can bring us suddenly to a potential growth-spurt. I believe with all my heart that God wants to use these moments to mature us spiritually, causing us to grow closer and more dependent on Him.

4. Have you encountered a "growth-spurt" experience(s) in your life? What was it (if you are in a group setting, you certainly do not need to share this out loud if you do not wish.)?

5. How did that experience(s) shape you or mature you? What wisdom did God add to you from that experience(s)?

6. Do you carry any emotional or mental scars from that experience(s)? How would you describe them?

7. Regarding these possible hurting areas in your life, how have you seen God working there?

Journaling Time

It's almost a cliché to bring up the man named Job when we speak about hardships in life . . . but here we go again. If you are not familiar with the story of Job you can catch up quickly as his stable, earthly life seemingly shatters in just 22 recorded verses. Read Job 1:1–22.

After losing everything, except a few servants and a really annoying wife, Job starts his "growth-spurt" experience with a declaration of worship in 1:21.

> *"I came naked from my mother's womb, and*
> *I will be stripped of everything when I die.*
> *The Lord gave me everything I had,*
> *and the Lord has taken it away;*
> *Praise the name of the Lord." (NLT)*

How can Job's wisdom inspire you in handling the future trials in your life?

My friend, as we age we will undoubtedly need wisdom. Not only in how to handle ourselves during trials, but everyday! What does James 1:5 assure us of?

James 1:6 attaches a stipulation to this promise. What is it?

Let's Pray . . .

Lord, Nothing I will ever go through is beyond Your understanding. There is no pain I could ever bear that is bigger than the healing You have to offer me. Thank You for being in control of my life. Thank You for holding me in the palm of Your hand.

Father, today I learned this:

Holy Spirit, remind me this week of these things:

Jesus, our relationship will benefit from these changes because:

Section Four

DISCIPLINE . . . THE TRILOGY

French Fries, Time Outs, and Tight Buns

> *"Oh the depth of the riches of the*
> *wisdom and knowledge of God!*
> *How unsearchable his judgments,*
> *and his paths beyond tracing out!"*
> *Romans 11:33*

Words carry such power. Just the sound of a word can change an attitude, make a pulse race, bring an old memory to mind, or end a fight. Words like summer, ice cream, pillow, and kiss, might bring a smile to your face and peace to your heart. Words like hate, cancer, thigh-master, and pap smear, might cause you to frantically hunt for an antacid. There's amazing power in words.

What does the word "discipline" do to you? Does it bring up memories of crazy things you did growing up and how you were deservedly punished by your parents? Does it make you smile to think of those days when you were discovering how far you could push the limits?

Or, does the word "discipline" make you nervous because the only discipline you received growing up was angry, hurtful, and shaming? Maybe someone in your past had a warped idea of how to discipline and you had to endure their abuse - verbal or physical. If that is what you have experienced, I'm so sorry. That is *not* how you were ever supposed to be disciplined. **That is not how our God disciplines us**.

In this section we'll continue to examine God's role of authority in our lives with a detailed look at God's discipline. Not much about God can be neatly tucked into a tidy package and His discipline is no exception. We will, however, take a gander at seven different types of discipline in hopes of better understanding His justice and His heart when it comes to chastening His children.

The questions are going to be set up a little differently in this portion of the book because you will have homework throughout the study, but there will still be room to journal your thoughts at the end of each chapter.

Girlfriends, please put your heart into this! There are parts that may take much thought and searching the scripture but God will bless you for your effort. You'll be asked to find people in scripture who serve as examples of God's discipline. God never changes and His truths are always fresh and alive. The way God worked in lives recorded thousands of years ago are still applicable today. You'll also be given the opportunity to pick out moments in your life where you underwent God's discipline - some that maybe you've never recognized before. These events are equally important because **you are God's modern day example**. It will help you see the way God has used discipline to shape you.

When you're finished traveling through this section, here are some things I hope you've picked-up along the way . . . maybe in the gift shop.

1. A deeper respect for God's authority.

2. A revelation of God's great concern and love for you.

3. A longing to accept discipline with humility and a moldable spirit.

4. A new godly perspective on your role as a disciplinarian.

"Discipline." You may never respond to that word like you do to "summer" and "ice cream," but you just might get to where you don't need to grab an antacid.

Chapter Ten

GODLY DISCIPLINE I

Reap What You Sow, Higher Authority, Domino Discipline

"Blessed is the man you discipline, O Lord,
the man you teach from your law . . ."
Psalm 94:12

When I was in elementary school we were not only graded academically but also on our behavior.

Any deficient area of conduct was marked with a bold, rather cocky, "I" which stood for, "Improvement Needed." Nobody was surprised that my report card faithfully strutted a cocky "I" in the area of "Controls Talking," but in the fourth grade things got a little out-of-hand. So much so, I even surprised my very own self.

Mrs. Rhonda Owens had bushy, brown hair and enormous glasses that dominated her smiley face. She was my fourth grade teacher and I loved her. Mrs. Owens seemed, at times, to be just one of the kids in the way she laughed at our antics and giggled at our jokes. Yes sir, it was great to have a teacher who really liked me . . . or so I thought.

Around the middle of my fourth grade year Mrs. Owens handed me my report card. I glanced at her face and saw no smiles there. Oh no! Intense panic gripped me as I tore open my report card, unknowingly about to unearth a conspiracy. My eyes zipped over my grades thinking they had caused the sorrow in my teacher-friend, but alas, they were fine. Stumped, I scanned over to my behavior grades expecting to simply say hello to my "I" in "Controls Talking." Instead, like trash littering the highway, this whole section was grossly plastered with "I's."

It seems "Controls Talking" had invited a cantankerous mob to join him in the "I" section. Their

names were nasty, like: "Works Well with Others,"
"Listens to Directions," and eight others whose
names are too uncouth to mention. As I began to
plan my own funeral, I checked the key at the top of
the card, making sure that "I" didn't suddenly mean,
"Incredible." No luck.

I couldn't look back at Mrs. Owens. I was jaded.
The only thing worse than letting Mrs. Owens down
was thinking of my parents' reaction when they found
out that I was nothing more than a juvenile delinquent
during the hours of eight to three every day. It was a
long, solemn walk home.

As it turned out, my mom and dad reacted quite
well to the newest revelation about their youngest
child. I didn't receive any gifts or anything, but I was
still allowed to live in their home, which I thought
was more than I deserved.

After discussing me with Mom, Dad said that
he and I would be eating French fries the next day at
a local restaurant. Now that probably sounds nice to
you, but to me, a doomed little girl with a great big
mouth, I knew it was sentencing time.

The ride to the old Pioneer Restaurant the next
day was pleasant enough, but as I looked out the
window I was appreciating what the outside world
looked like. I realized I was living on borrowed
time and probably wouldn't be seeing the free world

again for quite awhile. When we got to the restaurant my dad and I sat down in an old, worn booth and I listened to him talk, with wisdom and patient love, about the importance of controlling myself in class. Dad covered respect, listening, and the other nine misdemeanors while I ate my fries and cried. I was sure my Mom and Dad would go through the kid catalog and order a replacement.

Finally, my dad looked at my fries and me and delivered the verdict. For the next nine weeks, other than school, I was only allowed to play in my own backyard - which was the size of a small napkin. If, by the time the next report card came out, I could show proof of my rehabilitation by the purging those eleven "I's," I would be allowed to venture back out into civilization. I wondered to myself how I had become such a menace to society. Just a couple of days ago I was yucking it up with my old pal Mrs. Owens, now suddenly, I'm sucking down soggy French fries during my last few hours of freedom. Life is funny that way.

The good news is, the despair of disappointing my parents and my teacher were enough to immediately change my classroom etiquette. I learned to hold my tongue, even when I had a real zinger to throw in. I listened to instructions and even pretended to care about them. I smiled and nodded my head when Mrs.

Owens taught us stuff, even when I had no intention of learning anything. I was a changed girl! Not a good student, but a changed girl.

Convincing Mrs. Owens that I was "New and Improved" reached its perfect pinnacle on the day I saw little "Stephanie" come to reading class late without a place to sit. Seeing that there weren't any chairs available gave me an idea. Out of the corner of my eye I saw Mrs. Owens watching the situation. Seizing the opportunity I said, "Here Stephanie, take my chair."

As Stephanie took my chair I felt like Snow White in the forest - so pure and sweet that all the forest animals came to sing with her. I glanced over at Mrs. Owens and saw she was writing a note to send home to Snow White's parents informing them of my new refined, genteel way of life. I wondered if a note would be enough to gain my freedom. I also wondered if, once I had possession of the note, it would be safe to go push Stephanie out of my chair. After all, it *was* mine first.

Weeks of being sweet and thoughtful had really paid off. Shortly after this incident, my dad released me on good behavior. Not only was I free to roam the countryside with my new forest friends, but I don't believe I ever received another "I" on my report card. Oh, discipline isn't always pleasant, but when administered correctly, it can be life changing.

Mrs. Owens and my parents are not the only people who administer discipline. Listen to this rather long but beautiful passage about God's discipline. It's found in Hebrews 12:5–12.

> *"My son, do not make light of the Lord's discipline, and do not lose heart when he rebukes you, because the Lord disciplines those he loves, and he punishes everyone he accepts as a son. Endure hardship as discipline; God is treating you as sons. For what son is not disciplined by his father? If you are not disciplined (and everyone undergoes discipline), then you are illegitimate children and not true sons. Moreover, we have all had human fathers who disciplined us and we respected them for it. How much more should we submit to the Father of our spirits and live! Our fathers disciplined us for a little while as they thought best; but God disciplines us for our good, that we may share in his holiness. No discipline seems pleasant at the time, but painful. Later on, however, it produces a harvest of righteousness and peace for those who have been trained by it.*
>
> *Therefore, strengthen your feeble arms and weak knees. Make level paths for*

your feet, so that the lame may not
be disabled, but rather healed."

What a tremendous section of Scripture! So much information is camping out in that text we could go in a hundred different directions with it. To help us stay on track over the next three chapters, we'll focus on seven different kinds of discipline that we may encounter from our Heavenly Father—with or without the French fries.

You may find that some of these disciplines criss-cross each other at times. You may also find me repeating some crucial points again and again (I like to do that), in hopes that the truth will be branded in our minds for when we find ourselves under God's discipline. Are you ready? Let's get started!

I don't know about you but I commonly perceive God's discipline as harsh, dramatic, and intense. The thought of God punishing me instantly brings flashbacks of everything from locusts to leprosy, but this isn't usually the case. In fact, sometimes God disciplines us so naturally we overlook it all together. Because God disciplines those He loves it's good to train ourselves to be aware of His discipline. It's like cupping our hand over our ear to hear Him whisper, "I love you". The first discipline we'll cover is one often overlooked. I call it "Reap What You Sow" discipline.

R EAP WHAT YOU SOW

I would define this type of discipline as **a natural response to our choices**. It's when an authority over us seemingly surrenders us to our own choices. For instance, if your mother warned you twenty times not to climb a dangerous tree, there may have been a moment she decided to surrender you to your own choices. As you tumbled to the ground you should have realized that you were only experiencing a natural response to your poor choice. In the same way, if you choose to smoke for forty years you shouldn't be surprised when your health suffers from the effects of that choice. If you're a teenager having sex, protected or unprotected, don't be shocked or shake your fist at God when you end up pregnant, ill, or emotionally battered. If you choose to have sex outside of God's plan, you definitely will reap the natural consequences.

An example from the exciting life of Melissa: A very light example, that actually proves to be a heavy one, would be my constant battle with weight. I could blame the extra thirty pounds I carry (the extra thirty that I lie about on my driver's license) on heredity or having babies, but the truth is—it's Paul's fault. No, actually, I know the extra weight I lug around is a natural response to my choices in the way I eat and exercise (a lot of one and little of the other!). As long as I choose to eat like I do, I will carry extra weight. I reap what I sow. Nobody imposed these thirty pounds on me (except maybe the lady at the Cinnabon counter); it's a natural result of my choices.

God can use these natural results as discipline in our lives by making us come face to face with unhealthy choices. Will I listen to my mother? Will I continue to smoke? Will I continue to have sex outside of God's design? Will I continue to eat more than my body needs? God's hope for us, undoubtedly, is for us to begin to make healthier, wiser choices.

A Biblical Example: The first example I think of would be the prodigal son. In Luke 15:11–16, Jesus tells the story of a father with two sons. The older son served the father faithfully, while the younger son had some wild oats he longed to sow.

One day the younger son approached the father and asked for his inheritance now instead of later. I'm adding my own thought here, but I'm guessing this wasn't the first time this son made this request. Perhaps the father had denied him time and time again until finally he chose to release his son to his own poor choices. The happy, oblivious son went off with pockets full of cash. Life seemed great until, just a few verses later, we find this same child yearning to fill his ravenous belly with the pig's gruel he had been hired to deal out.

The Bible tells us this young man chose to blow all his inheritance on women, so-called-friends, and wild living. When his money was gone, so was everything and everyone else. As the foolish young man was about to fill his mouth with slop, he couldn't have possibly blamed his predicament on anyone else. He had chosen his path and now he had to **reap what he had sown.**

The father probably knew the outcome of his son's bad choice but he painfully allowed him to make a bad decision. Out of his great love, **he let his child experience brokenness from an unwise decision in hopes that he would someday become whole.**

Why didn't the father just say "No?" Why doesn't God just "zap" my extra weight off? Because a wise parent knows when it's time to let a child reap what he/she sows.

Now it's Your Turn!

Can you think of another biblical example of "Reap What You Sow" discipline?

Give an example from your own exciting life when you underwent "Reap What You Sow" discipline:

What did you learn from going through this experience?

HIGHER AUTHORITY

This discipline is very similar to the first. It also involves reaping what you sow. This one, however, is when **we experience a natural response of our choice(s) through the direct hand of a higher authority.** When we choose to speed, we get a ticket from a police officer that has the authority to discipline our actions. When we choose to cheat on our taxes, we will likely be disciplined by those in our government with the authority to do so.

An example from the exciting life of Melissa: I already shared with you the story of the eleven "I's" on my report card. In that situation I made the decision to be obnoxious in class and, as a result, I reaped what I sowed through the discipline of a higher authority.

Namely, Mrs. Owens and my parents. I'm not bitter, though.

A Biblical Example: Though there are many to choose from, I've always loved the story of Samson. It's a story that shows the holy power of God, the awesome power of Samson's strength, and the dangerous power of a manipulative, selfish, nagging woman. You'll want to (re)read this amazing saga, found in Judges 13–16.

Samson knew that the Lord made his hair the trophy of his strength and was never to take a razor to it. He also knew, from past experiences, not to trust anyone with the secret to his strength. Although he knew all this, in chapter 16 we find Samson gaga over a greedy woman named Delilah. Samson's Philistine enemies approached Delilah promising her great wealth if she could discover, and report to them, the source of Samson's strength. This devious woman went to work wearing Samson down until he finally, to prove his love, told her the source of his strength. What a fool! Delilah ran to the Philistines spilling the truth about Samson's hair and before you know it— Samson was bald, blind, weak, and enslaved.

Gracious! Samson made a choice to disobey God and what did it cost him? For one thing the Philistines plucked out his eyeballs! That alone was probably enough to make Samson swear off women but it also cost him his freedom, his strength, his great hair, and eventually, his life.

Samson is just one of MANY biblical examples of **discipline from a higher authority** in response to poor decisions, though he may have been one of the few to have his eyeballs plucked out. It makes me thankful I was only grounded for my fourth grade offense.

Now It's Your Turn!

Can you think of another biblical example of "A Higher Authority" discipline?

Give an example from your own exciting life when you underwent "A Higher Authority" discipline:

What did you learn from this experience?

DOMINO DISCIPLINE

Have you ever been punished because of the error of someone else? This makes me think of the effect infidelity has on a family. I'm presently watching this happen in the lives of a family I know. In this all too familiar situation, the husband has decided to turn his heart away from his family. Because of his hurtful choice, the husband is reaping heartbreaking consequences. If the heartbreaking consequences stopped at the guilty party it would almost seem justified, but instead, the painful penalties domino down the line.

First the pain of the affair hit this man's poor wife. Though she wasn't the one who strayed, depression, financial stress, embarrassment, and shame relentlessly cover her. From her, it traveled down to the children who have to deal with confusion, anger, and sorrow. The consequences continue to tumble right into the church, the community, and the extended family. Keep in mind; this is only half of the offensive party. The adulterous woman is "domino-ing" damage down her side of the world, as well.

So many people who are innocent of this wrong are harvesting hurt from the discipline wrought by two people. That's "Domino Discipline".

An example from the exciting life of Melissa:
Let me continue to regale you with another fourth
grade story of mine. For some reason, and I swear I
have no idea why, I drew an unflattering picture of my
beloved Mrs. Owens. By "unflattering", I refer mostly
to my controversial, artistic approach of drawing my
fourth grade teacher without any clothes on. I believe
I may have been trying to express how even our most
admired adults can find themselves to be unprepared
for the world around them—virtually naked in this
life! It was either that or the fact that my boyfriend sat
beside me and I drew it to make him laugh—yeah, I
think it was that one.

Well, somehow the unbecoming picture worked
its way into the snitching fingers of the smartest girl
in class who promptly shared the artwork with Mrs.
Owens. Luckily, neither the smart snitch nor my
teacher knew the identity of the artist, but as Mrs.
Owens held it backward to her soft tummy and sternly
said to the class, "Whoever drew this picture needs to
tell me right now," I about lost consciousness.

The only honest thing for me to do was to stand
up and confess! Looking back, I probably should
have done that.

Instead, up until this very day, I have never
confessed to the nudie portrait of Mrs. Owens. The
dominoes of my poor behavior ended in the entire

class having to stay in for recess the entire day. Did you get that? The whole class was disciplined for something I did! *At this point I would like to add a personal note: *If anyone from Mrs. Owens' fourth grade class is reading this, I'd like to say I'm sorry. Sorry to all of you except the little smart girl who ratted me out. Thank you.*

A Biblical Example: In Genesis 20, Abraham and his wife Sarah were moving but briefly stayed in a town named Gerar. Now, Sarah was beautiful. So beautiful in fact, that Abraham instructed her to tell people she was his sister for fear that someone would kill him to marry her. I find this story so ironic because Paul and I deal with this same problem when we travel (giggle-giggle).

Sure enough, the word of Sarah's surpassing beauty reached the king. King Abimelech sent for Sarah and brought her into his palace. Because of this offense, God disciplined the King and all the women in his household. During a dream, the Lord told Abimelech that Sarah was Abraham's wife and that Abimelech was **as good as dead** for taking her as his own! Can you stand it!?

You'll want to read this story to get all the juicy details, but the point is, the king and his household experienced discipline for something they were innocent of. Abraham and Sarah were the ones who were guilty of lies and faithlessness. Their decision dominoed discipline onto innocent people.

Now it's Your Turn!

Can you think of another biblical example of "Domino Discipline?"

Give an example from your own exciting life when you underwent "Domino Discipline."

What did you learn from this experience?

There you have it! The first three areas of discipline are under your belt. I hope that you have already seen that God's fingerprints are all over your life. God uses everyday experiences, good and bad, to shape us into the children He died for us to be. Remember, God disciplines those He loves, and Sister - He loves you so much! If He loves an uncontrollable, socially inept, little girl who draws nudie pictures, He certainly has an unquenchable longing for you.

Let's Pray . . .

Lord, Seeing Your discipline in my life is like seeing more evidence of Your love and concern for me. Help me to grow closer to You through any discipline that comes my way. Thank You for disciplining with justice and wisdom as I continue to mature in You.

Father, today I learned this:

Holy Spirit, remind me this week of these things:

Jesus, our relationship will benefit from these changes because:

Chapter Eleven

GODLY DISCIPLINE II

A Time of Waiting, A Time of Separation

*"The fear of the Lord is the beginning of
knowledge, but fools despise
wisdom and discipline."*
Proverbs 1:7 (NIV)

As a parent, discipline would be much easier
if my kids were all the same. However, because that
would have made things far too easy, God created

each child with distinctly unique needs, weaknesses, and responses toward discipline. Thank you, Lord.

In our relationship with God, because of our uniqueness, we may pass through these disciplines and not see every type of discipline used in our lives *so far.* That's okay, we're all different kids! The one thing regarding God's discipline in our lives that we will all have in common is that He faithfully disciplines with wisdom and justice. Because of this, we would be fools not to recognize His hand of authority and learn from His judgments.

So far we've looked at three types of discipline: "Reap what you sow," "Higher Authority," and "Domino Discipline." In this chapter, we'll cover our next two disciplines that involve waiting and separation. How about if we approach these like a kid approaches a cold swimming pool . . . let's just jump right in!

A TIME OF WAITING

"Wait patiently for the Lord.
Be brave and courageous.
Yes, wait patiently for the Lord."
Psalm 27:14

Years ago, during a two-hour road trip to visit my parents, my son Adam was particularly wound up.

I told him if he didn't settle down he would have to take a little nap when we got to Nanny and Poppy's. As sure as the sun rises and sets; my child also continued his predictable course. So as promised, when we arrived at Nanny's, Adam was sent off to the guestroom for a little rest.

After listening to his whining, groaning, and complaining, I said, "Now Adam, I want you to stay in this bed for a thirty-minute nap and then you can get up." To this, my usually very bright son said, "**No, not thirty minutes! Just an hour! Please, just one hour!**" I smiled and said, "O.K. honey, just an hour."

You see, at his young age, Adam had no concept of time. He didn't realize that he would have been better off to just trust me. Have you ever set your child down for a five-minute time-out and they respond as if you've said, "I'm calling off your birthday this year?" Desperately they scream, "No Mom! Not five minutes!" Then, while sitting on their time out chair with just a sliver of their buns, they squirm, complain, need drinks, need to potty, and fall off their chair. Watching this pitiful display you're thinking, "Kid, it's only five minutes. What's the big deal?" **The big deal is, children have no concept of our time.**

Are we like that? Surely not! This next form of discipline we'll explore is called, "A Time of

Waiting." **It's a point in our life, when despite all our attempts to speed things up, we just don't know what to do . . . but wait.**

> *"For a thousand years in your sight are*
> *like a day that has just gone by,*
> *or like a watch in the night."*
> Psalms 90:4

This verse is not one of great comfort to me while undergoing a time of waiting. I sit on the edge of my waiting-chair and say, "No Lord! Don't make me wait!" I squirm, complain, try to figure it out myself, fall down, and whimper. All the while my Heavenly Father must watch me and say, "Child, my timing is perfect. Just trust me." **You see my problem is, I just don't have any concept of God's timing.**

An example from the exciting life of Melissa:
Waiting is a station I visit a lot in my life. I'm a person who craves change. I like to try new things, start new programs, and daydream about new remodeling jobs in my home. However, what I hate to do - is wait. So, it only figures that I am even now knee deep in waiting.

Recently, I got the itch to move to a new home. I honestly never want to do anything outside of God's will, but sometimes it takes too long to search for it. My husband Paul would be content in waiting for a rock to go soft, but if I wait too long, I begin spinning my web of busyness and manipulation.

While waiting for news from the Lord about moving, I fill my time looking through home catalogs. I also make appointments with realtors, spread the rumor that we're moving, show people through our home, drag Paul to houses I want to buy, purchase paint for the new house, and send out change of address cards. I do all this and *still* feel uncertain to God's calling or aid.

Living this way feels like I'm grabbing the handle of a merry-go-round, running it in circles and trying to pick up speed. When I get it moving fast enough, I yell to Paul and God, "Hey, jump on! I've already got it spinning!" "Paul? . . . God?" Suddenly, I realize I'm running in circles **alone.** I'm dizzy, weary, and frustrated. Meanwhile, Paul is comfortably sitting under a shade tree waiting patiently with God.

When will I learn? When will I remember that God's timing is perfect? I want my life to be a display of God's guidance, not my own efforts. There's a time for acting on what God calls us to do - but I need to learn to wait for the call. By the way, you aren't looking for a new home are you?

The Lord knows my heart. Again, He knows

that I want nothing less than His perfect will for our family. It's just that I'm still learning to be obedient in my waiting patiently. I simply haven't grasped the concept of God's timing.

> **"Hey Lord, Whatcha doin'?"**
> **"I need a drink."**
> **"I want a cookie." "How much longer?"**
> **"I have to potty."**
> **"Can I get up now?"**

A Biblical Example: Let's use good ole' Abraham and beautiful Sarah again. God told Abraham in Genesis 15 that he would have descendants as numerous as the stars. That's almost unfathomable! Especially since Abram (later Abraham) was around eighty-five years old and childless with his seventy-six year old bride, Sarai (later Sarah), at the time. Tired of waiting, it was Sarai who came up with her own solution to the prophecy in chapter 16. We find her here, grabbing hold of the merry-go-round and running along side yelling, "Jump on Abram!"

"Take my maidservant Hagar. Sleep with her and maybe we can build a family through her." says Sarah. The Bible doesn't record Abraham putting up much of a fight against this idea, but that's another story. Abraham and Hagar did indeed have a son and this decision broke many hearts and deeply complicated the situation ("Reap what you sow," "Higher Authority," and "Domino Discipline" can all be found in this story). It wasn't until almost fifteen years later, when Abraham was one hundred and Sarah was over ninety, that their little Isaac was finally born. (chapter 21)

When I read this story I'm always baffled by the "Why?" Why did God make Abraham and Sarah wait so long? Plenty of scholars have probably figured this out but I always come to the same conclusion. God is God. He is much more concerned with the eternal than the temporary. Would we, over all these generations, have given God the deserved glory in this situation if this couple were in their blushing twenties? Would Abraham have been to the point of maturity that he was willing to follow God, even if it meant the death of his son? (chapter 22) No, I don't think so. **God sees the whole picture and His timing is perfect.**

Now it's Your Turn!

Can you find another biblical example of "A Time of Waiting" discipline?

Give an example from your own exciting life when you underwent "A TIME OF WAITING" discipline:

What did you learn from going through this experience?

> *"My son, do not despise the Lord's*
> *discipline and do not resent his rebuke,*
> *because the Lord disciplines those he loves,*
> *as a father the son he delights in."*
> Proverbs 3:11 & 12

A TIME OF SEPARATION

This discipline is distinctly different than "A Time of Waiting" because in a time of waiting you can still be in a growing relationship with God. However, when you experience "A Time of Separation" *you are unable to experience true intimacy with God.*

When I give my kids a time-out they may still be allowed to be in the same area with me. They like this because, although they're being punished, they can still see me moving around and watch what I'm doing. **My children would much prefer to sit confined in my presence than to be sent off to their room alone.**

Knowing the effect separation has on my children I sometimes discipline them by sending one off to his or her room for a time out. My hope in doing this is that the awkward feeling of being alone for a set amount of time, the separation, will bring them to repentance for the wrong they were guilty of. You see, **the separation is the discipline.**

I'm like my kids in the way that I'd much prefer to be waiting than to feel as if I'm separated from God. When I'm waiting for an answer from the Lord in my life, though I may not be getting that particular question settled, I can still see Him moving and working in other areas in me and around me.

The Bible says that "nothing can separate us from the love of God," and I believe that with all my heart. Nothing can separate my kids from my love either - but sometimes, *because of my love,* I will let them experience a time of being alone. When I send my child to their room I'm still in the house. I'm still keeping track of all they're doing but they can't experience my fellowship in the same way.

An example from the exciting life of Melissa:
The face of my relationship with God has been heavily freckled by feelings of separation or distance. When I start to feel this way, I first pray for the Holy Spirit to help me decipher if this feeling is a result of true discipline or perhaps a result of my being unfocused. Really, most of the time it has been laundry, hectic schedules, book deadlines, or hormones that have been the distraction rather than the discipline. These unfocused moments would be equal to our children watching television while we're speaking to them. They may be two feet from us but their focus is on that television and not on our telling them to pick up their socks. So ladies, sometimes a feeling of distance from the Lord may not be discipline but simply a need to shut off our distractions and turn our face towards our Father.

However, if my *feeling* of separation persists, I start to search through the rooms of my heart and pray that the Holy Spirit will open my eyes to anything I need to take care of spiritually. Sometimes upon inspection I've found old bitterness left lying around in the corners, hurtful thoughts lingering in the closet, and a basement full of careless words I have spoken. I need to get rid of those things!

*"How can I know all the sins
lurking in my heart?
Cleanse me from these hidden faults."
Psalm 19:12 NLT*

There comes a time when a mature Christian should know better than to fall into the traps of old sinful habits, time and time again. When I have been guilty of habitually turning toward a familiar sin (which has been more times than I can count), the Lord has turned me over to these habits, causing me to feel separated, until I chose to turn away from them and back to Him. **The separation was the discipline.**

A Biblical Example: I'm going to give you two types of separation examples: spiritual and physical. First, for the spiritual, let's look at Psalm 13 where we find David journaling about a time when he felt separated from his Lord. Watch carefully how David searches with frustration for the reason he feels separated but then beautifully falls back into his strong faith in mighty God.

*"How long, O Lord? Will you forget me
forever? How long will you hide your face
from me? How long must I wrestle with my
thoughts and every day have sorrow in my
heart? How long will my enemy triumph
over me?" Look on me and answer, O Lord
my God. Give light to my eyes, or I will
sleep in death; my enemy will say, "I have
overcome him," and my foes will rejoice*

when I fall. But I trust in your unfailing love;
my heart rejoices in your salvation. I will
sing to the Lord, for he has been good to me.

As for the discipline of physical separation, like sending our child to their room, we can find that God has done that to His children, too. Here is a rather harsh example found in Daniel, chapter 4.

King Nebuchadnezzar was full of blatant pride when the Lord physically separated him by placing him instantly, while in mid-arrogant-sentence, out in a pasture to graze on grass like a cow. Nebbie's body was drenched with dew and his hair grew like the feathers of an eagle and his nails like the claws of a bird. (vs. 33) The King stayed this way, physically and spiritually separated, until he finally acknowledged that God is the one who deserves the praise for any and all of his successes.

May I please have your attention! It's imperative that we remember that God does not discipline us out of a self-driven tantrum or boredom, nor does He separate us from His fellowship because He no longer loves us. In this discipline, we see that God separates us in hope that we will be overcome by the weight of our sin and repent. He wants us to choose to come back into fellowship with Him. **God always disciplines us for our good.**

We see God's great mercy in King

Nebuchadnezzar's continued story. Nebbie was restored to his throne and his kingdom and his position was stronger than ever before. The greatest mercy shown by God was the spiritual reunion between God and Nebechadnezzar. Read the king's own words in Daniel 4:36&37:

"When my sanity returned to me, so did my honor and glory and kingdom. My advisers and officers sought me out, and I was reestablished as head of my kingdom, with even greater honor than before."

"Now I, Nebuchadnezzar, praise and glorify and honor the King of Heaven. All his acts are just and true, and he is able to humble those who are proud."

This may seem like an extreme way for God to get King Nebuchadnezzar's attention, but I want to see it like Nebbie. He "woke up," spiritually and physically, to the realization that **God is a loving Father so full of love for His children that He'd do *anything* to draw them back to Himself.** He loves us so much!

Now it's your turn!

Can you find another biblical example of "A Time of Separation" discipline?

Give an example from your own exciting life when you underwent "A Time of Separation" discipline:

What did you learn from going through this experience?

    That concludes our study for today. Put your pencils down, and wait for someone to come and pick-up your papers. If you need a drink you may line up at the door.

    I continue to hope that you are learning to look for, and appreciate, God's discipline in your life. In our next study we'll wrap up the **Discipline**

Trilogy with the final two categories we're covering. Meanwhile, keep your eyes on your own paper and your hands to yourself.

Let's Pray . . .

Lord, I want to glorify You wherever I am physically or spiritually. I want to learn to glorify You while I wait by being patient and excited for Your certain response. In those times when I'm feeling separated from You, I want to glorify You by gripping hold of the **fact** of Your love for me. Thank You for Your discipline Lord.

Father, today I learned this:

Holy Spirit, remind me this week of these things:

Jesus, our relationship will benefit from these changes because:

Chapter Twelve

GODLY DISCIPLINE III

Verbal Confrontation, Spanking!

"I am the one who corrects and disciplines everyone I love. Be diligent and turn from your indifference."
Revelation 3:19

Five down, two to go! Together we have covered a plethora of godly disciplines. Don't you just love the word "plethora"? Gracefully tossing it into conversations makes me feel smart. Anyway, I hope you've enjoyed examining the handiwork of God's discipline in the lives of some favorite Bible characters, as well as in your own life. Some portions may have seemed scabrous, multifarious, or recalcitrant - but I hope you're having a good time. (I have no idea what I just said.)

We're ready now to look at the last two areas of discipline. These usually prove to be the harsher disciplines but one thing never changes in the spectrum of God's guidance - *He disciplines us with love for our own good and restoration.*

VERBAL CONFRONTATION

I hate verbal confrontation. Approaching someone in a confronting manner makes my insides turn like a tumbleweed. Even worse, if I think someone is going to confront me on an issue, I'm ready to tear my clothes and repent before I even know what I've done wrong - or even *if* I've done anything wrong. However, no matter how much I dread it, I can't deny that verbal confrontation is definitely a form of discipline God uses to guide and shape His children.

Godly verbal confrontation is an audible warning, either by God or someone sent by God, to caution you in the way you are heading or calling you to repent of something you have already done.

An example from the exciting life of Melissa:
The example I'm going to share isn't the harshest
verbal confrontation I've encountered but I'll use this
one because many of you will empathize with me. I
have, I guess you would say, an unhealthy attitude
toward my appearance. Sadly enough, this makes me
identify with nearly every woman holding this book
in her hand. My insecurity runs deep within me and
I've wrestled with it for many years. The strange
thing about a woman who feels negative about her
appearance, and I'm no exception, is that it cripples
nearly every area in her life. After allowing Satan to
use this insecurity to cripple me for so many years, in
so many areas, I feel as though I should be allowed to
park in the handicap spots at the mall.

Some time ago, I packed my bags and left for a
week-long Florida getaway with my best friends, Amy
Buck, Joey Mishler, and Shelly Weston. My opinion
of Florida is that it would be a far more enjoyable
place if it weren't for all the heat and beach spots. You
see, if I had the choice to get up and speak before an
audience of five thousand people or stand in front of a
few close friends while wearing a swimming suit - I'd
be out on that stage before you could say, "Cellulite."
Alas, there weren't any speaking offers for me that
week, but instead, loads of available beaches waiting
for my arrival. So, while my companions grabbed

their swimsuits and frolicked along the shore, I wearily grabbed my snowsuit (that's what the girls nick-named my beach attire) and pretended to be comfortable in the miserable heat.

One morning, Amy and I were out alone knee-deep in the ocean gathering sea shells in the quiet, early hours. Amy was sporting tiny shorts and a spaghetti-strapped top and I was decked-out in a cute pair of thermal pants and a turtleneck (not exactly, but you get the idea). After some quiet searching, Amy tucked one shell in her stylish little pocket and said very gently to me, "Missy, I hate to see you struggle with yourself like this." Her seriousness caught me off-guard and I looked at her face to make sure she wasn't joking. She wasn't.

I placed a few more shells in my parka and thought of how enslaved I felt by my self-obsession. For several moments we let the sound of the waves licking the beach fill the awkward silence. Then Amy gently spoke again, "Miss, you don't want Madison to grow up carrying the same attitudes you have about your body, do you?"

Ouch! I barely looked up at Amy. I usually enjoy joking about my summer wardrobe but it hurt to have the legacy I was passing on to Madison challenged. After all, I wasn't doing anything horrible! I wasn't smoking pot or having affairs. I wasn't even being grouchy about my body in front of my children. I had simply taken up a quiet hobby of hating pieces of myself.

Cocking up just the left part of my face, I mimicked a smile and defended myself to the Malibu Barbie standing before me. "Oh, Amy! I don't say anything negative about my body around Madison. She doesn't even know I feel bad about myself."

Reaching back down into the cool water and pulling out another shell, Amy said, "Missy, you know if Maddy hasn't picked up on your insecurities by now, it won't be long. Come on, you don't want her to judge herself as harshly as you do."

That conversation with Amy was short but it sunk its way deep into my heart. I knew I had a problem before Amy confronted me but her words were tools for change. Ladies, I want to make sure you understand the problem here. The problem was not my *beach attire*—I wholeheartedly believe God doesn't care if the world sees my chubby thighs or not. The problem was my *heart attire*. My heart, my relationship with God, was stifled by self-loathing in the way it kept me from accepting the beautiful and complete love God has for me. Not accepting that beautiful and complete love then caused debilitating effects on many other areas in my life. The most important area at stake, the one Amy pointed out, was the example I show to the little girl who will likely watch me closer than any other woman in her world. Also at risk was how my boys view women and their bodies. That conversation with Amy helped me see that it was time to change.

Another important aspect of this story is that Amy has been a cherished friend of mine for many years. Though she may not always be willing to admit it, I know she loves me and wants me to flourish as a person. Out of this love she challenged me on my sinful body-obsession. She didn't clobber me with hurtful words or threaten our friendship. ***Her words were truth and meant to be life-giving, not soul-draining.*** Let's re-read that key sentence, "Her words were truth and were meant to be life-giving, not soul-draining."

If we feel called to confront someone, it ALWAYS should be in God's life-giving love. *Anything else is suspect of having self-driven purposes.*

Hey, you know what? God's working in my life! Today, I'm much more forgiving of my bodily flaws and I speak unkindly to myself much less often. Bathing suits and I are still not friends, but Amy and I are! I'm so thankful for friends that care enough to be used as tools for God's transforming work in my life. My self esteem may always be an easy target for the devil to taunt me, but I'm changing. I'm transforming slowly, steadily, and surrounded by fabulous friends.

A Biblical Example: Read 2 Samuel 12:1–26. No really, go read it . . . I'll wait.

Here we find a perfect example of godly discipline in the form of verbal confrontation. David had sinned on several different levels with the taking of Bathsheba. David's arrogance and lack of self-control convinced him that lust, adultery, murder, and a list of other grievances, were somehow acceptable for a man in his position. God had other standards. Let's look at how God had Nathan, the prophet, approach David.

The first thing I want to point out in this story of confrontation is that Nathan was coming to confront David for one reason only; **God had sent him.** When we move on our own feelings, we are in danger of promoting our own agendas and not God's. Too many people run around like excited puppies with eager tongues wagging to confront others. **As far as I can see, chastening from the Lord will always be life-giving. The purpose of godly confronting should be re-building, not demolishing.**

Another great thing about God's confrontation through Nathan was the way Nathan captured King David's attention. **He approached him in a non-**

threatening way. I imagine Nathan coming boldly on God's behalf, yet humbly - knowing he was only a man himself. If Nathan had marched into David's court and yelled, "David, you're an idiot!" David's heart may not have reached such repentance so quickly—or ever.

Nathan, speaking the heart of God, laid out King David's sins like tree branches over a big pit. David easily took the bait and stepped right into the trap. Once he was in the pit, dug by his own tongue, there wasn't anywhere else to turn except to God. **The wrong was clearly defined,** in this case, by David himself.

The best part of God's confrontation is how it ends with a **choice of repentance and restoration.** The case of Nathan and David is no exception. Yes, David received punishment, but God took away his sin and restored David's relationship with Him.

God's example through Nathan and David is also an excellent model for us as parents when we confront our children with discipline, no matter what the age. Here it is again:

Be sure you are not disciplining for selfish reasons. Your words and discipline should be life-giving. They should be about re-building, not demolishing. Clearly define the offense. Encourage your child to do the defining. Try using an easy-to-

understand illustration to drive home the point. End your time together with an opportunity for repentance and assurance of restoration.

Now it's Your Turn!

Can you find another biblical example of "Verbal Confrontation" discipline?

Give an example from your own exciting life when you underwent (or were the delivery woman of) "Verbal Confrontation" discipline:

What did you learn from going through this experience?

"SPANKING!"

I'm calling this last discipline "Spanking!" because in my home the top-banana discipline you can receive is a spanking. When my kids leave their shirts on the floor, dishes in the basement, or break my favorite vase, they're not likely to receive a spanking. In my home a spanking is a punishment reserved for lies, habitual offenses, or a real doozie of a wrongdoing.

> *A* spanking received by God is a harsh discipline that leaves a lasting impression as the result of your sin or serves as a wake-up call to where you are heading.

My dad was the chief spanker when I was a kid. When I needed a spanking he would say four words that sucked every bit of moisture from my mouth: "Go get the paddle." Those words instantly made my face contort itself in dramatic displays of fear and trembling as I walked passed my smirking brothers.

I'm not sure why, but my brothers were always happy to see me get a spanking. It was like Christmas for them. I think they would have decorated for it had they been given more time to plan. As rotten as my brothers were, the worst part about a spanking actually was the paddle itself. The word "enormous" seems to best describe it. The size of that paddle, combined with the size of my father, sucks the moisture out of my mouth even as I type these keys.

Once I managed to drag the wooden paddle back to my parents' room I'd meet up with my dad who was waiting at the end of his bed. My dad never yelled at me before a spanking, he would only reach out and calmly take the burden of that paddle from my little hands and calmly talk to me about my offense(s).

"Now Missy, tell me . . ." Dad would faithfully begin the conversation, "why are you about to get this spanking?" Wondering if he had already forgotten, I'd blubber out the reason I was in this position.

"Do you understand why you were wrong?" Dad asked.

"Y - Y- Yes," I sobbed.

"Do you think you want to do that again?"

"N - N- No," I quivered.

At this point I'd always allow myself to grab hold of the slim hope that maybe, just maybe, Dad would see my remorse and announce that there'd be no spanking today - sort of a day of spanking-jubilee!

Instead, the words that fell from his lips were, "O.K. honey, lean over my lap."

Bending over was tough once the panic alarm in my body had gone off, making me automatically stiffen like a corpse. It took great effort, like bending a sheet of iron. When I finally was able to curve over my dad's extensive knees, I'd try to flex my buns as tight as a boulder so the impact would just vibrate up my dad's arm, like on the Bugs Bunny cartoons. That doesn't work, by the way.

My spanking was always one good swat on the bottom and the pain was never close to the dramatic ordeal of it all. After letting me cry for a short time my dad would pull my whole body into his hug and tell me how much he and Mom loved me. I told my dad, while inside his strong arms, that I loved him, too. Even though I was young I saw that spanking wasn't something my parents enjoyed. **I was spanked because I had made a choice to cross a well-defined line of behavior or action and had to pay the price for it.** I grew to understand that my parents loved me too much to allow me to live recklessly.

Paul and I try to follow the same basic procedure of spanking mapped out by my parents. **Spankings are not something that happen often. They are a reserved punishment that should never be angry, manipulative, or convenient.** If you are not an advocate of spanking, just substitute the name of this last discipline with your "top banana" discipline.

Whatever you choose to call it, the Lord also spanks His children. There are times when we, as His children, choose to cross a well-defined line of behavior or action and have to pay a price for it. Spankings may come after other forms of discipline from God or perhaps after a real doozie of a wrongdoing. **Keep in mind, as I continue to repeat over and over, that all discipline from God, even a spanking, is meant to edify us. To break us, yes, but hopefully to bring us to repentance and then to lead us to restoration.**

An example from the exciting life of Melissa: There are so many feelings, hurts, scars, and blessings involved in my next examples that if I don't make myself keep it short they would be a book in themselves. So, the short story is, one night I found myself in an unexpected position. I was sitting in front of a person I love who was crying and asking for my forgiveness for a wrong that was done to me. Immediately I said that I forgave, but the truth is, in the days and months that followed I ached so much that I spent a great deal of time hashing and rehashing things - growing angrier and more bitter. The more I thought about it, the more I realized I didn't really feel like forgiving this person. At the very least, I decided I could live with pretending to forgive while holding on to the bitterness to replay over and over in my head.

A little over a year later, I found myself in another unexpected position. As I told you a few chapters ago, I was involved in an automobile accident with a motorcyclist who was killed. Shortly after this accident, the son of the motorcyclist asked if he and I could meet. Preparing for that meeting was emotionally, spiritually, mentally, and physically exhausting. My greatest desire was to ask for his forgiveness and to receive it, but I had no idea what to anticipate. Many people were praying for this son and his family to be able to heal from the tragedy and also not to allow bitterness to take root.

The morning of our meeting, the young man walked quietly into the room where Paul and I were waiting. My insides felt hollowed out like a gourd. While I sat there, crying and longing for forgiveness, I underwent an unexpected, quiet spanking from God. Believe me, I was already so broken that it wasn't a terrible blow, just a deep sweep across my raw heart that allowed me to see that **I was asking for something I wasn't willing to give someone else.**

In my mind I instantly saw two chairs. I had been given the opportunity to sit in both seats: One, in the position of extending mercy—the other, in the position of hoping desperately to gain mercy. I was asking a person to show me forgiveness without bitterness. Was I willing to do the same?

God used this horrible event and my absolute brokenness as both a tool of discipline and a tool of growth. It has often been said that our greatest ministry will come out of our greatest pain and I have certainly found that to be true in my own life. The Bible promises us that in this world we will have trouble, but our hope rests in the truth that we have a God who has overcome this world! (John 16:32) His precious fingerprints can be found all over our tragedies in the lessons learned and the restoration of our souls. What the devil wanted to use to destroy us, God can use to transform, rebuild, and free us.

God was with me as I sat before the son of the motorcyclist. I did ask for his forgiveness and he did tell me he forgave me. I still pray for him as his heart mends from such an unspeakable loss. I've also been able to give my unforgiving heart and bitterness over to the Lord and have experienced much healing. God is so faithful.

A Biblical Example: Let's continue with the story of Nathan and David. (2 Samuel 12:1–25) God sent Nathan to tell David that because he repented of his sin, he would be allowed to live. However, because of the sin David fell into and the contempt it brought towards God, the baby born to David and Bathsheba would die.

At this part of David's story, I always feel compelled to stop and apologize for God. I want to say, "Now, I know the Bible says that God allowed this baby to die but let me just say, on God's behalf, that this incident is really not like Him at all! Normally, He's such a kind and loving God. I'm sure He'd like to forget this whole thing ever even happened."

Imagine my panic when David's story doesn't end with his baby's death. Because of David's flagrant sin with Bathsheba his life was plagued with trouble. God told David, "The sword will be a constant threat to your family . . ." (2 Sam. 12:10), and it was! David's daughter Tamar was raped by her own brother, Amnon. Amnon was then murdered by another brother named Absalom. Absalom later led a rebellion against David, his own father, and was killed in the battle. Even David's wives were sexually violated in public. On and on this dark cloud of havoc covered David's life and his descendants.

If God is good, how can this *purposeful* despair be explained? For me, as I've struggled through understanding God's harsh discipline, I've chosen to take peace in the fact that my mind is simply too small to understand the big picture God sees. Who am

I to question the ultimate mind of God anyway? Who am I to try to invent or market a God that I am more comfortable with? My opinion of God's discipline, in any form, is irrelevant because the bottom line is— God is God! I can not limit Him with my own limited thinking. Neither can you.

The real mystery is that this omnipotent, invincible, unstoppable God is, for some odd reason, so in love with us that He's willing to do anything to get our attention and transform us. God is always more concerned with our eternal wholeness than our temporary comfort.

Sister, if your eternal wholeness means sticking you in the hospital for a while so you'll finally look at the mess you're making of your life, I believe God would do it. He loves you that much! If your eternal wholeness means allowing you to be placed in a concentration camp, like Corrie Ten Boom, so that you, and millions after you, will know Him in a more intimate way, you can count on it. He longs for a relationship with you that much! If your eternal wholeness means being placed in a situation of grief and discomfort so you can learn the condition of your heart and the sin you cling to—I promise you, He'll allow it. He is unbelievably faithful at reaching us in ways we can't run away from.

God breaks us for temporary moments in hopes of restoring us for all of eternity.

After we have received our spanking, God will gather us in His great arms, allow us to cry for a while and then say, "You know child, I love you too much to allow you to live that way." God disciplines with justice for our good and His purpose. **God is so good.**

Please close this segment on discipline by reading Psalm 32 and 51. These are a couple of Psalms that David wrote after undergoing God's discipline. Make them a prayer in your own life.

Now it's Your Turn!

Can you think of another biblical example of "Spanking" discipline?

Give an example from your own exciting life when you underwent "Spanking" discipline:

What did you learn from this experience?

Let's Pray . . .

Lord, You are so holy. I'm thankful for Your discipline in my life. I also want to thank You for Your generous love and restoration available to me throughout my days. I love You.

Father, today I learned this:

Holy Spirit, remind me this week of these things:

Jesus, our relationship will benefit from these changes because:

Section Five

BOOGERS,
HEADLESS COCKROACHES,
AND A FRIED SQUIRREL

*"Don't copy the behavior and customs of
this world, but let God transform you into a
new person by changing the way you think.
Then you will know what God wants you
to do, and you will know how good and
pleasing and perfect his will really is."*
Romans 12:2 NLT

Do you remember the Transformer toys?
They're ugly, robot-looking things that only a boy
could appreciate. My boys tell me that a Transformer
is cool because if you carefully turn the arms up, the
legs down, the neck this way, and the nose that way,

it **amazingly** turns into another ugly, robot-looking thing. I'm glad I'm a girl. Transformers don't even come with their own little outfits or matching shoe sets. How depressing!

If you're a Christian, my friend, you too are supposed to be a transformer. Before you get offended, thinking I just called you an ugly robot, let me finish. God uses the time we have on this earth to challenge us to transform into being more like Christ. He uses events, people, scripture, discipline, and more - **to turn our eyes up, our mouth down, our knees bent, and our hearts around,** in hopes of transforming us into a reflection of Jesus.

In this last section we'll discuss the transformation process together. Chapter thirteen will have us look at how the things and people we surround ourselves with can influence our transformation. Then we'll flip-flop, in chapter fourteen, and study how we can best be used to influence those people around us during our own transformation process.

In our last chapter, number 15, we'll sort of sum it all up! You'll have time to journal new thoughts as well as look back through truths you've already gleaned. Perhaps you'll see some transforming God has already been doing in your heart and life.

All this talk of transforming has made me rather fond of those little robot toys. While you go on to the next chapter, I think I'll surprise my boys and sew their Transformers a dapper little suit with matching briefcase. What size shoe does an ugly robot wear, I wonder?

Chapter Thirteen

You're Surrounded!

*"Therefore, as God's chosen people, holy
and dearly loved, clothe yourselves
with compassion, kindness,
humility, gentleness and patience."*
Colossians 3:12 NIV

Do you know how a pearl is formed? The basics of this procedure were explained to me many years ago, but for the sake of accuracy I thought I'd brush up on my pearl-knowledge using my set of 1950 rummage sale encyclopedias. How much more could scientists have learned in just fifty short years anyway?

Let me share with you in a nutshell, or in an oyster shell rather, the process of making a pearl. According to my ancient information bank, if you were to take a special type of oyster and insert a simple grain of sand, or other small irritant, the oyster would start to secrete juices that stick to the little piece of sand. Over time this secretion hardens and begins to form yet another layer of secretion. This layering continues until eventually—Shazzam! You've got yourself a pearl. It may be a little more complicated than I've made it sound, but you get the idea.

My first thought about this process is how sickening I find the word "secretion." In fact, I seriously can't bring myself to suck on a Sucrets because the name is too similar. Perhaps it's this glitch within me that makes the practice of rubbing pearls on one's teeth to establish authenticity so revolting. You'd think by doing this "rubbing," you risk smearing some strange oyster's secretion all over your mouth. No thank you! Surely I'm not the only person to stay awake at night pondering such things.

Thank goodness I have other thoughts about this process. The exciting transformation within such an odd, unassuming shell also makes me think of what a tender Lord we have. He tucks beautiful reminders for His children to discover all over this planet to illustrate the great mercy, love, and grace He has for us. The extreme makeover of a worthless piece of dirt into a priceless pearl is encouraging. God can change the ordinary into the extraordinary; the common into a masterpiece. Hope abounds for all of us.

This all makes me think of another, strikingly similar, example of a transformation process. This particular "beautiful reminder" is tucked a little closer to home for us to discover together.

Go with me now in your mind to a beautiful, tropical beach. The sun is hot against your tan skin as you walk along the water's edge in your new black bikini (as long as we are imagining, I want to be in a black bikini! You can wear whatever you want.). As you walk along the shore, you allow your lovely toes to flirt with the cold, crystal-clear water.

Overcome with how stunning everything is, you suddenly throw yourself down on the toasty sand. Landing gracefully on the beach causes a few small pieces of warm sand to fly into the air. A tropical wind catches one of those little specks and takes it far into the ocean where it lands into the mouth of an oyster. Yet another grain of sand, a more unfortunate grain of sand, catches the wind and shoots itself straight up your nose. Unaware, you slowly get back up and continue walking along the beach to your house. (Yes girlfriend, you have a beach house).

As you go along through your day, a transformation is taking place to both of the charted pieces of sand—one, in the oyster; the other, in your nose. We're already familiar with the process of the oyster, but a little closer to home we have the second grain of sand also being covered in layers of secretion.

Your nose senses that there is a foreign object invading the cavity and so, to stop it from moving farther into the body, it begins to coat the little piece of sand with nose juices that harden over time. This secretion forms layers over layers until—Shazzam! You've got yourself a "booger." My encyclopedia doesn't cover the making of a booger but, because I'm feverishly driven in my pursuance of the truth, I called a nurse to verify the booger process. Although she validated my information, I may have lost a friend.

When these two grains of sand reach maturity in their places of captivity, they're finally ready to be harvested. While we won't go into the different harvesting techniques, we find that one sand is now a priceless pearl while the other sand is just a run-of-the-mill booger.

Out of fairness to the booger, let's remember

that the pearl does have a much longer gestation period. In fact, who's to say that this may just be the secret! Perhaps we're not leaving the sand in our noses long enough. Maybe if we kept it in there longer we'd all be rich. This must be what my kids are trying for; they're such entrepreneurs!

I'm aware how disgusting this whole conversation is but please indulge me; I really do have a point. The point is, though we have two similar grains of sand and two similar processes, the outcomes are completely different: a booger and a pearl. Just think of how unlike these two are. We would never see a wealthy woman brag about her new strand of gen-u-ine boogers while rubbing them across her teeth, would we? Likewise, I find it hard to hear myself yell to my children, "Stop wiping those pearls on the wall!" Isn't this ironic? Don't you find this outrageously intriguing?

Jesus used nature in many of His parables because people had a better chance of understanding heavenly truths when compared to things such as seeds, sheep, pearls, and sand. Although there are no recorded "booger parables" in scripture, I believe I'm really on to something. How can it be for two grains of sand to have such diverse outcomes? Let's dissect this parable one character at a time to find out.

Sand:

Both of our stories start with one identical property; sand. That's you and me. Psalm 103:14 says, "For he knows how we are formed, he remembers that we are dust." That verse is referring to Genesis 2:7 where God creates man out of what? Dust. Dirt. Sand. Even the music group, "Kansas," was aware of this fact when they sang the lyrics, "Dust in the wind, all we are is dust in the wind." God, Adam, and "Kansas" all realize that if left to ourselves, we're only capable of living as dust, or sand. We're here today; gone tomorrow (Ecclesiastes 3:20).

In saying that we're sand, I'm certainly not suggesting that we're not worth much. Good night, no! God gave up His own Son's life for common grains of sand like you and me. I'm pointing out the scriptural fact that our lives here are temporary and we, as people, are as numerous as the grains of sand on a beach. We're common.

Some people clutch the "common factor" a little tightly by seeing their commonness as bondage. They look across the huge beach of other grains and can't fathom that there's a glorious transformation available to them. With this handicap mindset, it's hard to see that God would ever hear your prayers, desire you for His child, or work through your life. It's easy to feel lost or overlooked, but rest assured, God sees us as unique individuals chock-full of purpose. Our mind may not be able to understand how He possibly could care about the entire beach but God doesn't ask us to understand His love, He just wants us to accept it.

Yes, we're like common grains of sand. God reminds us of this - not to depress us, but to keep our spirits in a humble consistency, ready to be molded by His artistic hands. Don't use your commonness as an excuse; God already knows who you are. On the other extreme, don't think higher of yourself than you should. Instead, be ready to be shaped into the image God sees as the perfect masterpiece for you.

Location:

Both stories continue with the identical sand being placed in a similar location. Though a nose and an oyster may seem completely different they are both simply moist, dark areas perfect for birthing beauties. We may think one location is socially more acceptable, but growth happens in both. When faced, once again, with promise of our transformation it's tempting to exchange our groaning about *who we are* (common sand) for groaning about *where we've been*. While it may be true that our growth was stunted by dysfunctional surroundings, WE ARE NOT STUCK THERE! Way back in chapter two we talked about how we can't let temporary things define us since we were created for the eternal. Friend, put your ear right up to this book so you are sure to hear me say this, "When you want God to take control of your life, it doesn't matter who you are, where you've been, or what you've done." 2 Corinthians 5:17 promises us, "If anyone is in Christ, he is a new creation; the old has gone, the new has come!" There comes a time in our transformation where maturity calls for us to let go of our past and cling to the beautiful hope of our future in Christ.

God is longing to catch hold of each of us, by the gentle blowing of His Holy Spirit, and draw us to Himself.

So, if it's not the sand and it's not the location that caused the extremely different outcomes in our parable of the booger and the pearl, then what is it? As much as I'd like to avoid the answer to that question, we must trudge onward. God seemed to place the real transforming power in what surrounded each tiny grain of sand. Dare I say it—the secretion.

Secretion:
Webster's dictionary defines secretion basically as a process of hiding something. When the nose or the oyster finds an intruder it begins to hide it by covering it, over and over again. The little sand inside

simply lays there, allowing itself to be covered, and **will ultimately be a product of the quality of what surrounds it.**

Your Heavenly Father's ultimate plan for you,
no matter **who** you are,
no matter **where** you're from,
no matter **what** you've done,
is for you to find rest in His presence
where He can begin to *cover you,*
surround you, hide you, and
transform you **in the richness of His glory.**

The process of God's changing the ordinary into the extraordinary takes time, but slowly, through a growing relationship with Him, we begin to be layered with the beautiful characteristics of Christ. Solid layers such as truth, righteousness, peace, and faith. (Ephesians 6:13–17) Life-changing layers like; compassion, kindness, humility, gentleness, patience, and forgiveness. (Colossians 3:12–13) Who we are and where we've been mean nothing because our God is limitless and will be faithful to complete His work in each one of us.

> *"He who began a good work in you*
> *will carry it on to completion*
> *until the day of Christ Jesus."*
> *Philippians 1:6*

God gives us a choice:

The choice of whether we would like to become a booger or a pearl seems like an obvious one, but it's easy to get caught up in the haphazard blowing of our days and be almost ignorant to all we are choosing to cover ourselves with. The devil is also in the transformation business. He loves to use *anything* this world has to tantalize us and cause us to casually, sometimes unknowingly, be coated with his layers of murderous secretion. Booger-quality layers such as lust, greed, prejudices, and a frightening tolerance of all sorts of worldly ideals. These layers harden our hearts and will slowly threaten to block out the blowing of the Holy Spirit and the voice of God.

"Be careful then, dear brothers and sisters. Make sure that your own hearts are not evil and unbelieving, turning you away from the living God. You must warn each other everyday, as long as it is called "today," so that none of you will be deceived by sin and hardened against God." Hebrews 3:12–14 NLT

Imitation Pearls:

There's another type of pearl that we didn't discuss and is probably the only kind of pearl I'll ever own. It's called the imitation pearl.

The imitation pearl looks very much like a

genuine pearl from a distance. Some are so well disguised they seem almost impossible to tell apart from the true pearls. According to my 1950's encyclopedia, the easiest way to discern a fraud from a genuine is to simply look around the hole used to string the bead for **chipped paint**!

Peeking under the paint of an imitation pearl you will discover a common glass bead. Manufactures extract a creamy liquid substance from fish scales (someone has *WAY* too much time on their hands!) and paint these beads to resemble authentic pearls. When these "pearls" are strung the paint often begins to chip. It doesn't take much rubbing on your teeth, or much wear and tear of any kind, to quickly reveal the truth.

Back in Chapter Five, "Vicarious Living," we studied together the importance of a genuine, personal relationship with Jesus Christ instead of living off someone else's experience or settling for a quick-fix. There are many basic truths I've repeated throughout this book in order to brand them into our thinking, hoping that we'll catch ourselves before becoming victims of a predictable spiritual felony.

Here again, with the imitation pearl, we see another example of the "quick-fix." People who want to *look* transformed without actually undergoing the work or time involved in the pearl-transformation.

They don't want to make life changes or die to selfish desires. They don't want to make the time to sit in God's presence and allow Him to cover them.

Matthew 7:15–20 warns us of imitation pearls. I'll bet we've all encountered people of this description or maybe we've even been one ourselves. The church is often a breeding ground for imitation pearls because of our confusion over what is true, transforming secretion. People who have grown up in the church and have spent their lives *surrounding* themselves with a list of acceptable behaviors and good deeds as a substitute for a personal relationship with God are imitations. Church, godly behavior, and good deeds are fine things, **but not in themselves** *transforming*. You might as well cover yourself with fish-paint. An "imitation pearl" might never miss a Sunday service or a pot-luck supper but the quality of what lies under their surface is revealed in the way they treat the unsaved, their willingness to help the needy, or their ability to forgive. The scratching of genuine Christ-life living may prove them to be only a booger at heart.

Remember, the quality of our transformation depends on whom and what we *surround* ourselves with. The layers of Christ will endure any kind of teeth-scraping trauma we must face. It is well worth the time and struggle.

Proverbs 27:19 says:
"As water reflects a face,
so a man's heart reflects the man."

Ladies, I don't want to be a booger. Have you ever seen someone's reaction when they see a booger? It isn't good. No matter how beautiful you have put yourself together, if you have a booger hanging out of your nose, nobody will remember your new dress! A person who claims to be like Christ but has a heart that says differently is just as disgusting to the eyes of God.

"They honor me with their lips, but
their hearts are far from me!"
Isaiah 29:13

Can I ask you something my friend? What are you **surrounding** yourself with? Are you purposefully **covering** yourself in God's word? Are you living your days with the intention of people noticing the beauty in your life? Living that way not for your own glory—you're only sand—but for the God who **covered** you in His beauty.

*Lord, I want to be so **hidden**, so*
***covered**, that when people look at me*
all they see are Your priceless layers.

Colossians 3:3 says,
"For you died, and your life is now
hidden with Christ in God."

Why don't you go climb in your own quiet, warm, (it doesn't have to be moist, although a hot bath sure sounds good!) place and allow the Lord to surround you with His wonderful arms. Let Him hide you in the shelter of His wings. Let Him cover you with His good and perfect will for your life. Come harvest time, you'll be a priceless gem.

Now that's something to rub your teeth on. Shazzam!

Surround Yourself

Chapter 13 Questions

Getting to know you,
getting to know all about you.

1. What is your favorite piece of jewelry?

2. Have you ever had to tell someone that they had a booger in their nose? Has anyone ever told you? How did you feel with either situation?

3. Would you rather have a vacation home on a secluded beach, a picturesque mountain, or a sprawling country-side? Why?

It's time to apply!

4. Have you ever used the fact that you are not yet a "pearl" as an excuse to pass up an opportunity to serve the Lord? What?

5. Do you like thinking about transforming or would you much rather just stay the same tomorrow as you are today? Why?

6. Read these next verses and note what kind of person God often uses for His service:

Luke 1:26–38 -

Matthew 3:4–6 -

Matthew 4:18–20 -

1 Samuel 16:7 -

Why does God often call people who are common, inexperienced, simple, and socially challenged? Read 1 Corinthians 1:26–31.

Read Matthew 9:16–17 and record anything that speaks to you about transformation.

Journaling Time

What do you spend an average day surrounding yourself with? Think about the television shows, movies, conversations, thoughts, internet, books, etc. that you choose to cover yourself with. Would you say these things surround you with good or bad "juices"?

Would you say that when people are with *you* they are being surrounded by good "juices"? (Your words, your attitudes, your habits, etc.) Why? Is there an area you may need to work on, if for no other reason, to aid in the transformation of others?

Remember the imitation pearl? Do you feel like your "Layers" can stand up to struggle because they are thick and strong, or are they simply chipping paint? Why?

Let's Pray . . .

Lord, I can't tell You how thankful I am that no matter where I've been, what I've done, or who I am - You still love me and want to transform me. Thank You for Your patience during my process. I love You.

Father, today I learned this:

Holy Spirit, remind me this week of these things:

Jesus, our relationship will benefit from these changes because:

Chapter Fourteen

GET REAL!

"Rejoice with those who rejoice; mourn with those who mourn. Live in harmony with one another. Do not be proud; be willing to associate with people of low position. Do not be conceited."
Romans 12:15, 16

Did You Know?

*A Jellyfish is 95% water. (There're certain times of the month that I feel like I am too.)

*Like fingerprints, everyone's tongue print is different. (The inkpad would be a little difficult to deal with.)

*You'll probably eat about 35,000 cookies in a lifetime. (I've always been an over-achiever.)

*A mole can dig a tunnel 300 feet long in one night! (I wish moles could get a job with the local road construction crews.)

*There are no words in the dictionary that rhyme with orange, purple, or month.

*An average size thundercloud holds about six trillion raindrops. (I didn't believe it, so I counted for myself . . . its true!)

*A goldfish has a memory of three seconds. (That's two seconds longer than my kids.)

*A hummingbird weighs less than a penny. (I'm running around $456.19.)

*The microwave was invented by a researcher who walked by a radar tube and a chocolate bar melted in his pocket! (If that were my pocket, I'd have thrown in a graham cracker and a couple of marshmallows.)

*Diet Coke was only invented in 1982.

*Porcupines float in water. (I hear they're replacing life vests on some cruise ships.)

*Astronauts can't cry in space because tears need gravity.

*Over 2,500 left-handed people are killed a year using products made for right-handed people! (Just helping you with your Christmas list.)

*There are more plastic flamingos in the United States than real ones.

*A hippo can open its mouth wide enough to fit a four-foot tall child inside. (So can I.)

*The average person has 1,460 dreams a year.

*A cockroach can survive without a head for several months. (Just another reason to hate them.)

*Most lipstick contains fish scales.

*Dolphins sleep with one eye open. (So will I after hearing about headless cockroaches!)

Ahhh, I love needless trivia. It makes me feel like I know something without really knowing anything at all. You know?

While dating Paul, my eyes were opened to elements of dating trivia I hadn't been aware of. I didn't know, for instance, that guys were only accountable to hold in their bodily gas for the first three months of dating. Apparently, the "Male Dating Handbook" clearly states that after the third month of exclusive courtship, the potential wife should be tested in her ability to cope with marriage to a "real man". While women may approach mate-selection by discovering views on children, religion, and future goals, guys place their trust in the "Flatulence-Reactor" test. If you're married, I guess the good news is—you passed! The bad news is this seems to be a life-long analysis. Good luck.

My Paul told me another little morsel of dating trivia that blew me away. He told me that there are girls who seldom get asked out because they're simply **too good looking**. First off, my immediate struggle with this new fact was that I obviously wasn't party to this elite category since Paul had already asked me out, but I tried not to dwell on it. My second struggle was the absurd unfairness of it all. Too good looking? That's ridiculous. I'd fight for this unjustness but it's a little difficult to overly pity these grotesquely beautiful people, don't you think? Let them fight their own battles.

You see, the fragility of the male ego shatters with rejection. Therefore, when ***too much beauty*** proposes ***too much challenge*** within the male mind, the male avoids the date proposal all together. It's astonishing that you can actually be so good looking that you render yourself unapproachable. ***It certainly doesn't do a girl, who is looking for a date, any good to be unapproachable.***

I know Christians who are unapproachable. To be honest, I've probably been one more times than I care to admit. Just as a pretty girl can present herself in a too-good-to-be-true fashion, we Christians often do the same thing. There seems to be a sick pride in presenting oneself as trouble-free. The problem is, while the unsaved world clearly recognizes the struggle in their own lives, we Christians walk around pretending our struggles are non-existent which makes us come across as out of touch and unapproachable. ***It certainly doesn't do a Christian, who is called to reach the unsaved, any good to be unapproachable.***

What good is an unapproachable Christian?

I was driving along listening to a Christian broadcaster announcing a guest coming on the show via telephone. As he painted a picture of this doting mother and altogether Super Woman I reached for my radio dial. I was in no mood to listen to some perfect woman drill me with guilt about all I'm not accomplishing (I have such a tender, teachable heart). Just as my fingers touched the dial I heard an obvious glitch in the show and I sat back to see what would happen.

Although the announcer had said, "Hi there and welcome to the show," there was no response. A long awkward silence smothered the airwaves until Super Woman herself let out the enormous roar of an irritated mother, **"JEREMY! Just give him back his pants! You *KNOW* those are NOT your pants!"**

Honestly, I couldn't breathe while mourning the instant this woman would realize she'd just bellowed at her kid in front of an audience of thousands. An awesome anticipation spilled over me. Both sympathy and hilarity dripped from my driver's seat as I sat waiting to see if this woman would cry, scream, or just hang-up.

The stunned announcer repeated her name

again and finally this fantastic guest caught on to what was happening and let out a great big laugh. The announcer and I joined her and I had to reach for the dial again. This time though, it was to turn up the volume so I could hear her speak over my own chuckling.

I actually gleaned more inspiration from the accidental "real life" moment than I did the event that earned this wonderful woman a spot on the show. I wasn't glad she was embarrassed - I've undergone enough embarrassment for all women to have a share. I was just suddenly reminded that this was a real woman, like me. In her bellowing she became approachable and I saw if God could use this real person, he could use me too.

There is something freeing about being ministered to by people who are willing to be real.

The apostle Paul wrote freely about his weaknesses in 2 Corinthians 12:9–10:

> *"But he said to me, "My grace is sufficient for you, for my power is made perfect in weakness. Therefore I will boast all the more gladly about my weaknesses, so that Christ's power may rest on me. That is why, for Christ's sake, I delight*

in weaknesses, in insults, in hardships,
in persecutions, in difficulties. For
when I am weak, then I am strong."

As Paul underwent his spiritual transformation he must have discovered that by being real, or approachable, he could be his most effective for Jesus Christ. To do this, Paul freely admitted his past—who he was, what he'd done, and where he'd been. For instance, Paul shares openly that he was a persecutor of Christians (Acts 22:1–20). He tells of his struggles with sin and temptation and how he finds himself doing the things he doesn't want to do (Romans 7:14–25). He even expresses the heartache of being stuck with a physical ailment that he longed to be healed of but never, in this life, received (2nd Corinthians 12:7, 8). Ephesians 3:8 is my favorite though. Here Paul puts his face right in mine and says with intense honesty, "I feel like I am less than the least of all God's people."

When I read Paul's God-breathed words in scripture, I see that he was in the transformation process just like me. The beauty of Paul's ministry is often found in his willingness to say, in essence:

"If God can love me, He can love you."

"If God can forgive me, He can forgive you."

"If God can use me, He can use you."

There is something freeing about being willing to be real.

On a personal note:

There's a conundrum within me. While I know I'm called to speak and minister to women, I also know how much work there is to be done in my life. I struggle every day with temptation and usually end up losing. My mouth operates more fluently than my brain so I'm constantly saying things I shouldn't. And, not to beat a dead horse, I'm also selfish, manipulative, and often critical. You may be reading this thinking, "Well, then why am I reading your book?" My point exactly! Why would God want to use me when I'm such a work in progress?

The words of Paul and countless other scriptures, several we covered last lesson, have helped me realize the types of people God pours His power into.

People with an appalling past.
People with emotional scars.
People with physical handicaps.
People who are simple-minded.
People who are poor, dirty,
and foul-smelling.
People who used to brim with hatred.
People who are addicted to self.

People who seem useless to society.
People who fail everyday.
People like me.

Thank the Lord, He uses people like me.

You know what I'd like to grasp hold of once and for all? I'd like to remember that God has called me to a transformation journey and He wants to use me every step of the way. He wants to use me just how I am today, not how He hopes I'll be tomorrow, or next week, or next year. *He can use me in spite of myself.* He can use my stunted vocabulary, silly stories, and vocal range the size of a tic-tac. The most effective person I will ever be *along my journey* will be as someone who is real *about her journey*. Someone who is approachable and leaves people with the hope and truth that:

"If God can love her, surely He can love me."

"If God can forgive her, surely He can forgive me."

"If God can use her, surely He can use me."

To be honest, I've not fully grasped this yet. I still like to look better spiritually than I actually am. That's just normal; we all like to look good. But friends, what good would I be for the Lord if I chose to be unapproachable? Now let me hop out of the hot seat and ask you that question? What good are you for the Lord if you choose to be unapproachable? We can either be honest about ourselves and our struggles in this life, or we can wait and knock-the-socks-off people when we all stand before God. Why not knock-some-socks-off now by looking people in the eye and relating on their level, hoping to make some eternal differences.

One person bent on making their self appear too-good-to-be true can be hurtful enough, but fill a big, pretty building up with hundreds of them and now we've really got problems! I deeply love and respect the church and hope not to sound like a church-basher, but surely we are all aware that most of the world doesn't feel particularly at ease in a church building. It's actually not the church building people don't like - it's just the church people they don't care for. You probably are also aware that many churches have grown too comfortable with only appealing to the "churched" and have left the others to find something else. When the attitude of a church gets to this point, they have rendered themselves unapproachable. It certainly doesn't do a church who's hoping to bring people to Christ, any good to be unapproachable.

Matthew 9:10–13
"While Jesus was having dinner at
Matthew's house, many tax collectors and
"sinners" came and ate with him and
his disciples. When the Pharisees saw
this, they asked his disciples, "Why does

your teacher eat with tax collectors and 'sinners'?" On hearing this, Jesus said, "It is not the healthy who need a doctor, but the sick. But go and learn what this means:

'I desire mercy, not sacrifice.' For I have not come to call the righteous, but sinners."

Did you catch the beauty in that passage? These "sinners" approached Jesus and His friends while they were eating. **What was it about Jesus that made the spiritually sick feel comfortable approaching Him? What is it with the majority of churches today that make the spiritually sick feel sicker?**

A reporter decided to do a special on alligators in the Everglades. The writer/photographer decided he would not merely write about alligators—he would become one!

The brave reporter headed off to the Everglades for his alligator rendezvous armed with his camera and a two-foot stick. He found a swamp known for its large alligator population and began to walk carefully into the murky water. His movements were slow and calculated, until finally, he found himself looking eye-to-eye with all the scaly alligators that surrounded him.

There, in the swamp, the reporter stood for hours observing the alligators and carefully taking pictures. When the alligators moved, he moved. When the alligators went underwater, he went underwater. At times the huge reptiles would come over to him to get a closer look and the reporter would gently push them away with his stick. This went on until the dedicated man was satisfied with his work. Finally, he turned around and slowly made his way back up onto dry land. With my luck, I would have arrived on shore and discovered I'd left the lens cap on.

As you can imagine, the photographs and the observations made by the journalist that day were life changing. His work was heralded "A Revelation!" because *instead of standing safely on shore, he grabbed a stick and dove in for a different perspective.* He looked his mission in the eye and related on its level.

To be truly effective for our Lord we need to make our way down into the swamp; into the water where the world is drowning. The best way of doing this starts with personally deciding to be **real.** Making the choice to look hurting people in the eyes, going under when they go under, taking them by the hand and offering them words of hope about One who has been there before. By getting on the level of those around us, God can use us as "A Revelation!" in the furtherance of His work.

There is something freeing about a church who is willing to be real!

Hebrews 4:15 says, "For we do not have a high priest who is unable to sympathize with our weaknesses, but we have one who has been tempted in every way, just as we are - yet was without sin."

Why was it so important to God's plan that Jesus be allowed to undergo temptation in every way we ever will? Was it so we can feel alienated by the fact that Jesus never failed? No, it was so that . . .

" . . . we can then boldly approach the throne of grace with confidence, so that we may receive mercy and find grace to help us in our time of need."(vs.16)

Our God is approachable! When we are tempted we can approach Him with confidence, knowing He understands. I believe He will look us in our eyes and say, "I know it's hard, I've been there too. Friend, in this world you'll have all sorts of trouble, but don't lose hope! I've overcome the world." (**based on John 16:33b**).

There is something freeing about loving a God who is real.

There's a lot of needless trivia out there that's just as useless to us as living unapproachably. Today, however, I hope God has opened your eyes to truth. The truth of what it means to live effectively by being willing to share about your journey - along your journey, with all who cross your path. Keep transforming and use the lessons and wisdom you glean along the way to share with others. Ask God to show you those He wants you to share with. Oh, one last piece of advice, be sure to pack some chocolate in your pockets for the road . . . it's bound to be a long haul.

Get Real!

Chapter 14 Questions

Getting to know you,
getting to know all about you . . .

1. Have you ever had to get rid of cockroaches? How'd you do it?

2. Where were you when Diet Coke was invented in 1982?

It's time to apply!

God wants to transform us. As we trade-in our weaknesses for His strength, our failures for His perfection, our sin for His forgiveness - we can witness to those around us through the reality of our own transformation process. By being real and approachable we show that if God can transform us, He can transform anyone.

3. Would you consider yourself a person who is easily approachable? How do you know that?

4. Who, in your life, is a Christian role model to you? Are you comfortable sharing your weaknesses and struggles with that person? Why or why not?

5. Would you consider your church a place where people feel free to share their weaknesses and struggles? If yes, what are you doing, as a church, to

be so approachable? If no, what could you do, as a church to be more approachable?

*If you are in a group setting, be careful of your discussion. Find a way to be truthful without bashing your church.

Journaling Time

6. Read Proverbs 25:20 and journal what this says to you about being real with people.

7. When was the last time you looked a hurting person in the eyes and related to them on the same level?

To be approachable, or real, doesn't mean that we walk around wearing a t-shirt that says, "Hey, I struggle with pornography, come and talk to me about it!" It doesn't mean we write across our foreheads, "My husband is an adulterer" or "I'm a huge gossip." Struggles and hurts can be very personal and we don't need to spray them around like cheap perfume to be qualified as approachable. Oozing such things would actually be repelling.

How about instead we start every day asking the Lord to open our eyes to someone that needs to be seen. We'll ask Him to help us see past the surface answers and cheesy smiles into the real need in her life. Then, we need to be willing to re-adjust our schedules to this person's need and pray for the Lord's wisdom in what we share.

Remember these things as you minister:

1. God will not ask you to speak to a man, other than your husband, pastor, or counselor, about ANYTHING personal. If you know of a need in a man's life, go and tell a male pastor or other mature Christian man.

2. God, as far as I know, would not want you to air someone else's dirty laundry. That's gossip. If you

have gone through hurt involving another person and you see God wanting you to share it, get permission from that other person first. If that isn't possible, be in prayer about a way to share your experience without unveiling the other person(s) involved. If you share this any other way, you may have continued healing to do and may be bent on rehashing old bitterness. There are things I've decided I will never speak on again because I have found this true in my own life.

3. On the other end, if God leads you to someone and she tells you personal hurts and struggles in her life, you need to be a woman who will hold the burden for that person without phoning it as a prayer request to some friends. God will be faithful to hear your prayers without the aid of a few close buddies. Unless that woman is in danger, keep your mouth shut and her secrets safe.

4. Lastly, and I must share this because I'm a Mom, be careful about who you speak to. Don't go anywhere with a stranger. Don't get into trouble sharing personal things over the internet. Wash your hands after you potty and look both ways before you cross the street.

Being real isn't something we can bottle up and manipulate into a chapter or two. It's an awareness of making the most of each lesson learned, each person encountered, and each word spoken throughout the day. It's a process like most others - one you fail at and try again. But please, do try.

$\mathcal{B}$e vulnerable instead of shallow; Honest instead of surface; Eternal instead of temporary.

There is POWER in *reaching out.*

There is POWER in *recycling* all God has brought you through.

There is POWER in *being real.*

*****

"Because he himself suffered when he was tempted, he is able to help those who are being tempted."
Hebrews 2:18

*****

This last section will not be shared as a group. This is for your own journaling privacy but is an insightful look to at all God has done in your life, all

He continues to do, and what He may (or may not) want you to do with it.

List the top three lessons or trials that you have gone through in your life so far:

1.

2.

3.

Now list how you are changed because of what the Lord taught you in those events.

1.

2.

3.

Pray that the Lord will use the wisdom and insight He gave you to help further his Kingdom here on earth. Pray specifically in one or all of these areas, or come up with your own.

1. Lead me to A WOMAN *in my church* that can benefit from my experiences.

2. Lead me to A WOMAN *outside my church* who can benefit from my experiences.

3. Prepare me to be open to what or whom you will bring my way.

4. Give me discernment and wisdom of how much to share about my experiences.

*****

Let's Pray . . .

Lord, You're so approachable! It's refreshing to know that Your Son went through every problem and temptation I go through. I want to praise You for understanding my hurts and struggles, and I want to thank You for Your willingness to stay with me while I make every effort to heal, grow, and transform.

Father, today I learned this:

Holy Spirit, remind me this week of these things:

Jesus, our relationship will benefit from these changes because:

Chapter Fifteen

SUMMING IT UP!

*"Give honor to the Lord for the glory
of his name. Worship the Lord
in the splendor of his holiness."*
Psalm 29:2

While stepping out of the bathtub, I heard a tremendously loud sound. BAMMM! I ran to the window to look outside not knowing whether to expect a blown-up car or Chef Emeril kicking his cooking up a notch. Instead, all I could see was my neighbor searching for the source of the blow as well.

Deciding my nudity would cause a bigger upset

than any explosion, I chose to get dressed before venturing out into the yard to join my neighbor. By the time I was decent, the bombing suspect had already been found out. It was a squirrel.

Now, I'm not an expert on electricity, but I guess when this squirrel decided to hide a few nuts in the circuit box up on the electric pole in my backyard, he not only shorted out the electricity to the tune of a thunderous "BAMMM!" but he also fried himself and his dinner!

My neighbor left me standing over the poor, stiff squirrel lying on the grass under the pole. As I studied him I couldn't help but strangely identify with his demise. I softly said, "I know how you feel Mr. Squirrel." You see, this rodent had ventured so close to the source of power that he ended up overwhelmed and nutless. I feel that way sometimes.

Seeking God's purpose for your life, whatever season you're in, *is a good thing*.

Being spiritually challenged to fall deeper in love with God *is a good thing*.

Humbly accepting God's role of authority in all areas of your life *is a good thing*.

Looking at how God's discipline shapes a believer *is a good thing*.

Focusing on your journey of being spiritually transformed *is a good thing*.

God is faithful to open our spiritual eyes when we ask. He can use our temporary days to add eternal wisdom to our souls. Out of simple silliness He can address attitudes and habits that mangle our spiritual appearance. If you have turned your heart to Him through the various studies of this book, then I have no doubt that He has shown you some truths to spiritually consider. He has shown me many areas, through the writing of this book, that hold back my own transformation. Like I said, He is faithful.

Taking a look back over the last fourteen chapters will be *a good thing* as we revisit the truths God has shown us. *It also may be overwhelming*. When we hold our lives up to the holy reflection of Christ's example we may feel like a fried squirrel. Being so close to the Source of Power can make our inadequacies seem too much to face, leaving us feeling burdened with all the work ahead of us.

However, the Lord says in Matthew 11:28,

"Come to me, all you who are weary and burdened, and I will give you rest. Take my yoke upon you and learn from me, for I am gentle and humble in heart, and you will find rest for your souls. For my yoke is easy and my burden is light."

Where should we start? Maybe as you look back across the simple lessons of this book you see that God is already at work transforming you. That's awesome! But if you still see a whole mess of work ahead of you, don't worry. The best part of the transformation process is that God doesn't expect us to change all at once. It's not like slipping on a new coat. It's more like wearily breaking in a new pair of shoes. When we love the shoes enough (or spent too much money on them to throw them away) we endure the foreign feel and the blisters until finally they become shaped to our own foot and wear like second skin.

When God brings a weak area to your attention, He will always show you a better way to live and will give you a healthier, life-giving garment to adorn your character and transform you. Keep these truths close by so you can remember them and ask a friend to hold you accountable in case you want to give up when you hit a "blister."

The most important thing you can do as you transform - which is for the rest of your life - is to faithfully meet with the Lord. This truth can not be repeated enough because it's absolutely essential to every area in your life. I keep these words of David in Psalm 28:8 taped on the side of my dresser in order to be reminded each morning of the importance of this one-on-one relationship:

> *"My heart has heard you say, "Come and meet with me." And my heart responds, "Lord, I am coming."*

Take time right now and ask for the Lord's guidance as you thumb back through the chapters. Look at each chapter just long enough to have the main thought come to your mind. When you grab that thought, think of how the Lord may want to use this truth in your own life and jot it down in the space provided.

Chapter 1: "Seasons of Life"
Main thought:

What this means in my life:

Chapter 2: "Identity Crisis"
Main thought:

What this means in my life:

Chapter 3: "Eternal Refreshment"
Main thought:

What this means in my life:

Chapter 4: "Love Letters"
Main thought:

What this means in my life:

Chapter 5: "Vicarious Living"
Main thought:

What this means in my life:

Chapter 6: "Spiritual Senses"
Main thought:

What this means in my life:

Chapter 7: "Mixed-up Thinking"
Main thought:

What this means in my life:

Chapter 8: "Not Enough"
Main thought:

What this means in my life:

Chapter 9: "Wisdom Worth Aging For"
Main thought:

What this means in my life:

Melissa Jansen

Chapters 10 - 12: "Discipline!"
Main thought:

What this means in my life:

Chapter 13: "You're Surrounded!"
Main thought:

What this means in my life:

Chapter 14: "Get Real!"
Main thought:

What this means in my life:

James 1:22–24 speaks to the heart about transformation:

> *"Do not merely listen to the word, and*
> *so deceive yourselves. Do what it says.*
> *Anyone who listens to the word but*
> *doesn't do what it says is like a man*
> *who looks at his face in a mirror and,*
> *after looking at himself, goes away and*
> *immediately forgets what he looks like."*

Friend, thank you. It's been such a joy traveling through this book together. I've been praying for you, and will continue to pray for those who read this study, to be encouraged in their journey of transformation. Since I've got such a long way to go myself it's nice to know I'm not traveling alone. Let's keep trudging along remembering that God is for us. He's cheering us on! The love He has for each one of us is tremendous and humbling.

Let's close in prayer.

Lord, thank You for each woman reading this book right now. Thank You for her beauty, her tender heart, and her desire to become more like You. Please continue to draw her close to Your side and whisper in her ears Your desire for her to grow, transform, heal, strengthen, and bring You glory. Let her remember any truth You have revealed to her in these pages and keep her coming back to Your waters for refreshment. What a joy it is to know You Lord! What a privilege it is to be Your daughters! Amen.

Alrightie gals, thanks again. It's nice to find ladies who'll walk beside me, ***even when I have toilet paper stuck to my shoe.***

Love,
Melissa
Jansen

Contact Melissa Jansen
or order more copies of this book at

TATE PUBLISHING, LLC

127 East Trade Center Terrace
Mustang, Oklahoma 73064

(888) 361 - 9473

Tate Publishing, LLC

www.tatepublishing.com